GREGYNOG

GREGYNOG, THE PRESENT HOUSE

GREGYNOG

EDITED BY

GLYN TEGAI HUGHES

PRYS MORGAN

J. GARETH THOMAS

CARDIFF
UNIVERSITY OF WALES PRESS
1977

ISBN 0 7083 0634 9

Printed by Qualitex Printing Limited, Cardiff

CONTENTS

CONTENTS

ILLUSTRATIONS

EDITORIAL NOTE

DETAILED acknowledgements are to be found in the individual chapters and the notes attached to them. The editors, however, wish to express their general indebtedness to the many who have helped in the production of the book, not least to their fellow contributors. The opinions expounded are naturally individual ones and are, no doubt, none the worse for that.

Saesneg yw iaith y llyfr gan mwyaf, ond hyfrydwch oedd cael adargraffu Cymraeg cyhyrog Ifor Williams a W. J. Gruffydd.

CHAPTER ONE

GREGYNOG — THE REGIONAL SETTING

HAROLD CARTER AND J. GARETH THOMAS

GREGYNOG is located in that region of Wales which is generally called 'The Middle Borderland' (Figure 1). Of all the Welsh border country this middle area epitomizes the physical and human characteristics of a border region in geographical terms. The uplands of Central Wales extend long fingers of land to the east, such as the Long Mountain and the Kerry Hills, while also in this same region tongues of riverine lowland reach westwards far into Wales, as in the Upper Severn, or Vale of Powys, near which Gregynog lies. This is also a region in which after many centuries of conflict two peoples and two languages have reached a situation in which although each strives to maintain its identity, both also integrate into a region which is essentially transitional in character.

Three elements make up the physical character of this part of the Middle Borderland. The first is the lowlands of the east, generally 200 metres (or about 600 feet) in altitude, opening into the Shropshire plain where Shrewsbury dominates as the regional capital, and gradually narrowing westward along the river lowlands where there is a series of smaller towns which are almost equidistantly spaced. The second element is the highland and moorland reaching to well over 400 metres (1,350 feet) in height and forming the mountain core of Mid-Wales. Between these two elements lies the third, a series of plateau-like surfaces falling away to the east and presenting smooth unbroken skylines, the dominating surface being between 250 and 300 metres (800 and 1,000 feet) high. These three elements are clearly demarcated on Figure 1 (whilst in the extreme west the summits of Pumlumon and the Berwyn Mountains appear at altitudes of over 600 metres (2,000 feet)).

The greatest proportion of valley lowland, apart from the Shropshire Plain itself, is related to the areas draining directly to the Severn, for not only do these include the well developed flat floored valleys of the Vale of Powys (the Severn west of the Breiddens, the small upland area marked on

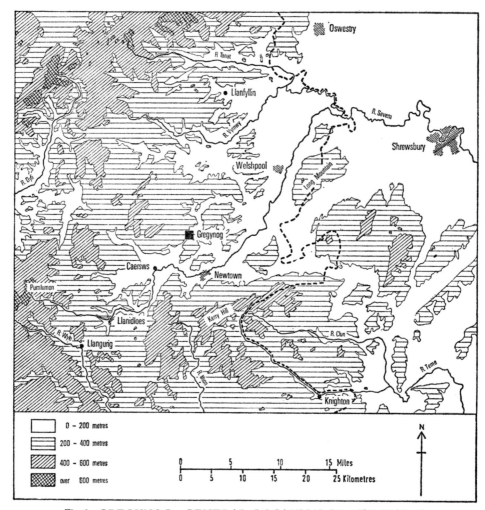

Fig. 1 GREGYNOG: GENERAL LOCATION IN MID WALES
The Welsh-English border is indicated by a heavy broken line

Figure 1 north of the Long Mountain), but also those of Dyffryn Meifod
(the river Vyrnwy) and other sizeable rivers such as the Tanat. These
rivers in turn break up the continuity of the transitional plateau element
so that it appears as a series of blocks fringing the western highlands.

Gregynog itself is located in the very heart of this middle borderland
in the area where the wide expanse of the Severn valley floor becomes
attenuated and where the intermediate plateaux therefore dominate the
local scenery.

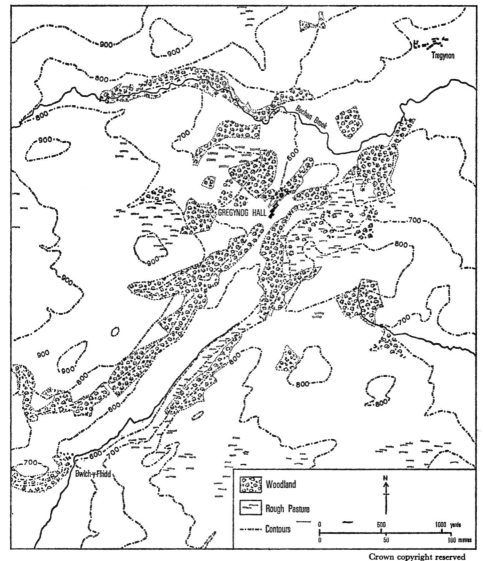

Fig. 2 GREGYNOG: SOME SITE FEATURES

Figure 2 indicates the local topography and the site of Gregynog itself. The first feature is the domination of the area by the plateau surface at 250 metres (between 800 and 900 feet) for, as may be seen, level extents at these altitudes characterize the greater proportion of the map. The small streams that drain off this surface have eroded small but quite deep valleys into it and these are shown by the sharp re-entrants. The second feature is that Gregynog itself is located in a very distinctive through valley which extends from Tregynon in the north east through to Bwlch-y-Ffridd in the south west. This is not an unusual feature in the area although it is not easy to explain. It is possibly due to erosion working along a line of geological weakness, but whatever the cause the result is a fairly steep sided valley to the south west which opens out onto the 'watershed' of the through valley on which Gregynog itself is located. To north west and south east the ground rises to the plateau surface and it is these wooded slopes which dominate the site of the house itself and break the view from its windows.

The land use and vegetation of the area parallel the altitudinal and physical characteristics. The narrow valleys are dominantly wooded, especially along the steeply sloping sides. At the highest levels of the plateau summits at 275 metres (over 900 feet), there are extents of rough pasture, whilst patches of furze occupy the slopes and intermingle with the moorland. In between, the bulk of the area is under farmland. Gregynog itself is in a typically wooded valley although most of this woodland is, of course, planted woodland and is therefore well landscaped.

It could well be argued that Gregynog occupies a symbolic borderland location. In general terms it is within the transitional zone where lowland gives way to upland as the Welsh mountains are approached. In a detailed context it occupies a site a little above the small eroding tributaries of the main river and a little below that level surface which dominates the intermediate zone. On a small level interfluvial area it stands as an effective symbol of the area in which it is located.

The borderland location is emphasized by the relation of Gregynog to the Welsh language divide, that area of rapid transition which separates Y Fro Gymraeg or Welsh Wales from the predominantly Anglicized areas of the Borderland. Table 1 shows the proportions of the population over the age of three able to speak Welsh by parishes along a direct east-west line through Gregynog from the English border to the west coast. Two features stand out. The first is that the frontier of Anglicization has pushed west beyond Gregynog, but the Hall still lies within that rapid zone of change where the percentages fall sharply from somewhere above seventy to below ten. The second feature is that the changes between 1961 and 1971 show the major conflict area just to the west of Gregynog in the parish of Llanwyddelan. To west and east there is relatively little change. It can be argued, therefore, that the symbolic physical location is to a degree reflected in a cultural context for although it is located very much on the eastern edge of the divide between Welsh speaking and English speaking Wales, nevertheless it occupies a point within that broad band where the change takes place.

TABLE 1

Percentage able to speak Welsh at 1971 Census.
A Cross Section of Montgomeryshire* from East to West

	Parish	1971	Change 1961–71
East	Forden	7.4	0
	Berriew	6.1	+0.3
	Tregynon (includes Gregynog)	16.7	—0.5
	Llanwyddelan	33.3	—18.2
	Llanllugan	71.9	—4.9
	Carno	82.4	—6.3
	Llanbrynmair	85.9	—2.3
West	Darowen	89.5	—2.3

*The administrative county prior to 1 April 1974

As will be appreciated from the above description of its overall physical location Gregynog is situated in a region which is predominantly agricultural in economy and rural in social and settlement patterns. It is true that the lead bearing lodes of the slopes of Pumlumon at one time provided an important mineral resource, but with changes in world supply and demand these became uneconomic to mine after the first world war, and by the 1920s production in even the largest of these undertakings had been discontinued. The lead bearing area was in any case west of Gregynog and even when lead mining was at its peak, the effect upon the economic and social life of the region immediately surrounding the Hall was minimal. Nor indeed was the effect upon the settlement pattern of the middle Borderland as a whole very marked. With two or three exceptions the lead mines were small undertakings providing an additional source of employment and income in an economy which remained agricultural, rather than themselves creating new settlements, be they town or village, which were industrial in origin or in character.

The agricultural economy of the region has always been that of mixed farming, with an emphasis upon animal rearing—an emphasis which derives inevitably from the general altitude of the region, from its westerly location in Britain and from the heavy acidic and leached boulder clay soil with which it is overlain. Store cattle are, therefore, reared on the uplands whence they move down to the more lush valley pastures for fattening or for developing as dairy herds. Neither of these cattle rearing activities gives rise to any industry as such, although of course their attendant commercial requirements are concentrated in small market towns such as Welshpool, Newtown and Llanidloes. The one agricultural activity which did in fact give rise directly to the development of industry in these towns, particularly in Newtown and Llanidloes, and to a lesser extent in some of the larger villages, was that of the sheep farming which was and is so typical of the higher plateau surfaces. It was the wool of these sheep which gave rise to the tall smoke stacks of the woollen and flannel mills which rise so incongruously over the roof tops of Newtown and Llanidloes, and though they are now smokeless they gave Newtown in the nineteenth century the nickname of 'the Leeds of Wales'.

Once again, however, after a production peak in the late nineteenth century, changing fashions and a combination of economic circumstances led to the region's inability to compete with the West Riding of Yorkshire and its once thriving woollen industry went into a decline from which it has never recovered.

When the Misses Davies entered into possession of Gregynog just after the end of the first World War they were taking over an estate in a region which was virtually devoid both of extractive and of manufacturing industry. It is true that there was some quarrying of local stone for building and road metal purposes but as employers of labour in the region as a whole, such activities were minimal in their effect. There was also a small manufacturing and processing element in the employment structure of the towns, e.g. tanning and leather processing, and in Llanidloes a metal foundry which having initially been linked to the making of machinery for the lead mining industry had successfully adapted itself to the manufacture of mining equipment in general. The labour demands of these activities however, were easily met by the towns in which they were located, and the effect upon the surrounding countryside was negligible.

The social and economic structure of Gregynog's surroundings was therefore based on agriculture, and based moreover upon a type of agriculture which by its very nature was not labour-intensive. In this structure, leaving aside for a moment the market towns, there were five major elements.

The first, and most numerous of these was that of the farming community itself. The one aspect of this element consisted of tenant farmers, either of estates like Gregynog itself, though the number of such tenants was limited because such estates were relatively small, or more frequently of larger estates whose 'headquarters' were outside the region itself, e.g. the Londonderry estate. Many of these tenant farms were in parts of the area which had been enclosed, and the farms created, by the Enclosure Acts of the late eighteenth and nineteenth centuries. Much of the territory immediately to the south of Gregynog through its rectangular fields and straight wide lanes bears witness to the effect of these Acts upon the landscape. The other aspect consisted of the owner-farmer, the so-called 'yeoman-farmer' whose status in society, both self-induced and generally recognized, was much higher than that of his tenant neighbour who was so often condemned to dealing with his landlord through the proxy of a seemingly all-powerful 'agent'.

The second element was directly linked either to the yeoman farmer or tenant farmer and was that of the farm labourer, either 'living in' if single, or occupying a farm cottage if married and with a family. In those days of course such an occupancy was a 'tied tenancy' and it could be terminated at the whim of the employer, with results, in some circumstances, which are best left to the imagination.

Closely associated in economic and social conditions and in status with the farm labourer was the third element, namely that of the person who was a direct employee of an estate and of the house which it supported. Here, of course, the range of employment was wider since it included interior domestic posts as well as those concerned with the maintenance of grounds, gardens, parks and woodlands. The social status was also different since no head gardener or keeper on an estate would in any way regard as an equal the cowman on the home farm or on the farm of a neighbouring tenant of the estate. There was, however, no basic difference in the fundamental conditions under which they held their employment.

The fourth element was naturally the service element in the community, be it in the public sector, e.g. education and other Local or Government services or in the then private sector, e.g. the medical, nursing and legal professions.

In one way or another, the first three of these elements were directly or indirectly linked with the fifth aspect of the social structure of the region, namely that of the estate owners themselves. This element was only really effective if the owners were actually resident in the region, and this is what happened in the case of Gregynog. In presiding over Gregynog in person, and in taking a direct and personal interest in its affairs the Misses Davies were in fact, though probably unintentionally, acting as major employers of labour, and Gregynog was as important to the general economy and welfare of its immediate hinterland and of its inhabitants as is British Leyland now to Cowley or Margam to Port Talbot, although of course, on a different scale. During the inter-war years therefore, Gregynog, in common with other major estates in the region, was in bald economic terms an income-generating institution and as such was a key element in the economy of the area.

In the social and cultural sense, the contribution of Gregynog at this time to the life of the region was no less effective, though it had much wider implications. The Misses Davies were not Welsh speaking, and their education had been in the context of a broad Western European culture rather than in that of Wales as a small cultural unit within that broader sphere. Their good works were therefore geared to the improvement of social and economic conditions in Wales during the Depression, rather than to the furthering of the cultural health of the nation as such. Thus it was that while their philanthropy and generosity were applied and appreciated in the depressed areas of South Wales, in furthering medical education in the Principality as a whole and in supporting, in very generous manner, local charities and services which at that time were dependent upon voluntary contributors (e.g. hospitals and District Nursing Associations), their cultural activities were in a broader context. Chairs of International Politics, of Geography and Anthropology, and of Music for example are those which they founded, not of Welsh Literature, Welsh History and Celtic Studies. It was the French Impressionists whose paintings graced the walls of Gregynog and it was the music of Bach, Handel, Mozart and Beethoven, performed and conducted by eminent international musicians, supported by a choir drawn from estate workers, which resounded through the Music Room at the Easter and Summer concerts to which local people were invited. The impact upon such people therefore was to introduce them to live performances and direct viewing at a time when travel to exhibitions or concerts was financially prohibitive and when radio reception was no less inadequate in that part of Mid-Wales than it is at the present time. In terms of direct employment Gregynog's effect was local but in those of more general philanthropy and of contributions to cultural and educational matters its effect was both regional and national.

The war of 1939–45 of course put an end, though not immediately, to the special contribution which Gregynog had made to the life of that part of Montgomeryshire (now Powys), and to Wales as a whole. Ever since the early years of the century, with the decline of the woollen and mining industries, the region had become one of depopulation through migration. The employment offered by estates such as Gregynog had played its part in helping, in a small way, to offset this need for outward migration but in the post-war period, for economic reasons, their role in this context was very much reduced. Indeed, they virtually ceased to be significant job-suppliers and together with the increasing mechanization of a system of agriculture that was not labour-intensive, added yet another impetus, though in a negative and involuntary sense, to the outward movement of young people which has had such a disastrous effect upon the demographic, economic and social health of mid-Wales in general and of this region in particular.

When the University took over full responsibility, with vacant possession of the house, in 1963, it was acquiring what had in Wales come to be regarded as virtually a national institution because of its contribution to social, economic and cultural matters in the Principality, and one which had exerted a considerable and direct influence upon the life of its immediate region. In all senses, however, save the physical, the institution had become one of past glory because although the house and estate were still being maintained, virtually on a care and maintenance basis, Gregynog was no longer able, in the changed social and economic conditions of post-war Britain, to operate as a great national charitable and cultural foundation. In some instances indeed it was no longer necessary, with the introduction of the Welfare State, for it to do so. It was partly a feeling that Gregynog was no longer fulfilling a useful purpose that had led Miss Margaret Davies, motivated as she always was by a deep sense of responsibility to society, to experiment with one or two ideas for its use before deciding to offer it to the University.

The University, therefore, as a formally constituted national Institution, took over what, albeit in a more limited context, had been another national, though privately financed, institution, one based on patronage in the best sense of the word. In doing this the University has assumed responsibilities of three very different kinds.

In the first place it has operated Gregynog, under the terms of the deed of gift, as a residential educational centre corporately for the Constituent Institutions of the University. Secondly it has endeavoured and is endeavouring to maintain the cultural and less formal educational traditions of Gregynog not only in the context of Wales as a whole but also specifically in that of Powys. Thirdly it is endeavouring to operate the estate and the house itself neither as an institution nor as some latter-day local squire but as a modern employer of a varied if limited labour force thus enabling Gregynog, as in the past, to make a direct contribution to the economy of its hinterland. The way in which these responsibilities are being discharged will be described in more detail in some of the succeeding chapters.

CHAPTER TWO

GREGYNOG

IFOR WILLIAMS*

I

Y N y rhifyn diwethaf o'r LLENOR, ceryddir fi gan yr Athro W. J. Gruffydd am ysgrifennu *Gregynnog*, yn lle *Y Gregynnog*, yn enw'r Wasg gelfydd o gyffiniau'r Drenewydd. Dywed mai *Gregynog* oedd y ffurf arferol nes i Syr John Morris-Jones gywiro'r hen ffurf mewn dwy ffordd—(1) rhoddi dwy *n* yn lle un, a (2) rhoddi'r fannod o flaen yr enw. Yna â ymlaen, 'Yn awr, yn enw pob rheswm, paham y cadwyd y gwelliant cyntaf (y gellid dadlau yn ei erbyn gyda pheth tebygrwydd), ac y gwrthodwyd yr ail welliant, na ellir dadlau yn ei erbyn ar unrhyw dir yn y byd, mwy nag y gellir dadlau yn erbyn *Y Rhedynnog*, *Yr Eithinog*, ac felly yn y blaen. Yr wyf yn gobeithio yr eir yn ôl yn y llyfrau nesaf at ffurfiau cywir Morris-Jones.' Gan fod y nodyn hwn mor bendant y mae perygl i bobl ei goelio, a gresyn fyddai hynny, gan mor anghywir ydyw! Ni wiw i mi ddweud mewn geiriau plaen fy marn i amdano, gan fod yr Athro Gruffydd yn perthyn mor agos i Olygydd Y LLENOR. Ymfodlonnaf ar ddweud yn syml fy rheswm am newid y ffurf.

Gan fod cynifer o enwau treigledig ar arfer, megis *Faenol*, *Weun Galchog*, nid oedd dim yn annaturiol mewn tybio bod *Gregynog* yn dreigliad o *Cregynog* (gw. mynegai i waith L. G. Cothi, 505, er mai *Gregynog* yw'r ffurf, td. 431, nodyn; ni ddigwydd yn y cywydd), a daeth Syr John i gredu mai 'lle â llawer o gregyn ynddo' oedd y meddwl. Felly newidiodd yr enw. Dangosodd ein llyfrgellydd Dr. T. Richards i mi y ffurf *cregynog* yn *Llythyrau'r Morrisiaid*, i. 355, enw William Morris ar ei gist gywrain i ddal cregyn, neu gregin. Enw Cymraeg y Wasg, pan ofynnwyd i mi olygu Sallwyr Dr. Morgan, oedd *Gwasg y Gregynnog*, a gofynnodd y cyfarwyddwr i mi a oeddwn yn cytuno â hyn. Cyn ateb, chwiliais cystal ag y medrwn mewn byr amser yn y cofnodion, a'r ffrwyth oedd hyn,—cefais ugeiniau

* Reprinted from *Y LLENOR*, ix, 4 (Gaeaf 1930), 225–33, by kind permission of Hughes & Son (Publishers) Ltd. This article by the late Sir Ifor Williams, with its reply from the late Professor W. J. Gruffydd, are followed by an exposition with additional commentaries by the late Professor Melville Richards. See below, pp. 18–24.

o enghreifftiau o'r enw yn y ffurf *Gregynog*, heb fannod, a chydag un *n*;
a'r rheini yn tarddu o adeg pur gynnar yn yr unfed ganrif ar bymtheg.
Ni ches ond un enghraifft o'r *nn* (gw. *Mont. Coll.*, ix, 309, prydles yn
1638–9 i 'Arthur Blayney of *Gregynnogg*'): ni ches gymaint ag un *Y
Gregynog*. Parodd hyn amheuaeth am yr hyn a eilw'r Athro Gruffydd yn
'ddau welliant'. Tybed mai dau gamgymeriad oeddynt? Ar ddamwain,
trewais ar *Grugunawc* mewn cân na allai fod lawer diweddarach nag 1150
(yn wir yr oedd rhywun wedi achub y blaen arnaf, gw. *Mont. Coll.*, iii,
224). Nid oedd bannod o'i flaen; ac un *n* oedd ynddo, ond gan fod
cymaint o lawysgrifau yn rhoi *Celynog* am air y gwyddwn fod dwy *n*
ynddo, ni fedrwn bwyso ar yr ail bwynt. Ond yr oedd absenoldeb y
fannod yn bendant a therfynol, pe medrid profi mai'r un lle oedd â'n
Gregynog ni. Yn ddiweddarach daeth y prawf o hynny hefyd i'r amlwg.
Nid oedd dim i'w wneud, ond hysbysu cyfarwyddwr y Wasg fod yn
rhaid dileu'r fannod—yr oeddwn yn sicr o hynny,—ond nad oeddwn yn
sicr am y ddwy *n*, ac felly y peth gorau oedd gadael llonydd iddynt, nes
cael goleuni pellach. Am y tarddiad, ni wyddwn ddim, ond tybiwn y
gallai ddyfod o enw dyn oherwydd bod *Grugyn* yn digwydd yn Llyfr
Aneirin fel enw un o'r Gododdin, a hefyd yn chwedl Cilhwch ac Olwen.
Dyna oedd fy marn ddwy flynedd a mwy yn ôl: wedyn bu raid i mi leddfu
peth arni, fel y gwelir isod. Y ffordd y mae'r ffeithiau yn fy arwain bellach
yw i gyfeiriad yr un *n*, gyda goddefiad i *nn*.

'Ond,' meddai un o'r Llenoriaid, 'onid yw yn gywilydd o beth na ŵyr
athrawon Cymraeg sawl *n* sydd mewn gair?' Efallai, wir. Cymerer yr
Athro Gruffydd yn enghraifft: ysgrifennodd yn y nodyn a ddyfynnais
uchod na ellir dadlau yn erbyn *Y Rhedynnog*. Gellir. Yn Llyfr Coch Hergest,
un o'n llawysgrifau safonol, ceir a ganlyn (R.B.B. 335), 'aeth cofeint
ystrat flur y *redynawc* velen yggwyned,' h.y., aeth cwfaint neu dylwyth
mynachlog Ystrad Fflur i *Redynog* Felen yng Ngwynedd. Nid oes fannod
o flaen yr enw (arddodiad yw'r *y*, heddiw 'i'), ac un *n* sydd ynddo! Felly
hefyd M.A. 633*a*; cf. hefyd freinlen Aberconwy, *Redenocuelen* (*Hist. Aber.*,
165); a'r *Record of Caernarvon*, td. 43, *Redinokuelen*. Dengys y ffurfiau
cyfatebol mewn Gwyddeleg (*raithnech*), a Llydaweg Diweddar (*radenek*),
yn arbennig yr olaf, mai un *n* oedd yn y famiaith. Gweler ymhellach
Eiriadur Davies, 1632, *rhedynen*; T. W. ar 'filictum,' *rhedynos* (cf. Gr. C.
144, *rhedynossydd*). Rhydd *rhedyn*, *-en*, *-og* (td. 102). Nid y terfyniad *-ynn*
sydd yn *rhedyn*, mwy nag yn *telyn*, ac ni ddyblir yr *n* wrth chwanegu sillaf.

Ond y mae gwaith yr Athro yn dyblu yn *Rhedynawg* yn dangos yn glir beth allai copïwr llawysgrif ei wneud, neu'n wir lafar gwlad ardal, neu genedl, sef dyblu *n* trwy gydweddiad â gair hysbys. Ar ddelw *Celynnawg* hawdd iawn fuasai i'r iaith lafar, a'r iaith lyfr, ysgrifennu hefyd *Rhedynnawg*, er nad oedd ond un *n* yn yr olaf o'i darddiad. Dyna pam y credaf y gellir esgusodi *Gregynnog*. Yr oedd lle o'r enw *Celynnog* yn rhan o feddiant teulu Gregynog, ac yn ymyl y plas. Nid syn fuasai i'r ddau derfyniad effeithio ar ei gilydd.

Rhof yn awr y prif gyfeiriadau at yr enw. Y cyntaf yw marwnad Cynddelw (1150–1200) i feibion Dwywg (*Myv. Arch.*, 184). Geilw hwy, 'Keidweid greid *grugunan* lys.' Llinell gyntaf yr englyn nesaf yw

> *Grugunawc* eryr *grugunan* gynnetyf.

Deallaf hyn i olygu bod yr arwr yn eryr neu arglwydd *Grugunawc*, a'i fod o'r un gynneddf neu anian â rhyw wron o'r enw *Grugunan*, y gŵr a roes enw i *Grugunan lys*. Digwydd yr un enw ym mreinlenni Llandaf (gw. L.L., 155, 240); un o'r tystion yw *Grucinan*. Dyna'r ffurf mewn orgraff hŷn lawer nag un Cynddelw: terfyniad bachigyn yw -*an*, fel yn *Manawyd-an*, etc. Gedy hyn *Grucin*, ond nid oes sicrwydd beth all ddigwydd i -*in* ar ôl *u*, nac ychwaith yn niwedd gair, a thybio mai *in* ydoedd y sain. Ond yn yr hen orgraff saif hefyd am -*yn* yn ein horgraff ni. Y mae *Grugin* a *Grugyn* yn bosibl. Rhaid trafod yn nes ymlaen y modd y cafwyd *u* yn yr ail sillaf.

Y prawf dros ddal mai'r un lle yw *Grugunawc* Cynddelw â *Gregynog* y Drefnewydd yw hyn: bardd o Bowys oedd y Prydydd Mawr, ac i wŷr Powys y canai yn bennaf, ac mae Gregynog ym Mhowys. Tyst yw ef i'r ffurf heb fannod, ac yn dechrau ag *G* mor gynnar â'r ddeuddegfed ganrif. Yna, mewn llawysgrif o tua 1550–60, o waith Lewis Morgannwg, Gruffudd Hiraethog, a Wiliam Llŷn, tri bardd, tri achwr cyfarwydd, hysbys yn nhraddodiadau teuluoedd, rhoir achau tylwyth Ieuan Blaenau, hynafiad hen berchenogion Gregynog, ac yno ceir tystiolaeth i'r lle, a'r enw. Dyfynna Dr. Evans (R.W.M., i. 823, ar Peniarth 132), deitl ach Dafydd Llwyd Blaenau, perchen Gregynog yng nghanol yr unfed ganrif ar bymtheg:

> *Kydewain*, tref gynon, *yneuadd yngrvgvnoc*.

Enw'r plas yn Saesneg oedd Gregynog Hall: yn Gymraeg y ffurf, yn ôl

beirdd ac achwyr 1550, oedd *y Neuadd yng Ngrugunog*. Hynyna am y ffurf.
O blaid mai'r un lle a olygir, cofier bod Gregynog ym mhlwyf Tregynon,
a bod Tregynon yng Nghydewain. Ni roir bannod o flaen yr enw
Grugunog gan Gynddelw tua 1150, na chan y beirdd hyn tua 1550. Ac
ni chefais fannod chwaith yn Gymraeg na Saesneg yn Lewis Dwn, na'r
cofnodion a ddyfynnir yn y *Montgomeryshire Collections*. Perchen y Neuadd
yng Ngrugunog, pan luniwyd yr ach, oedd Dafydd Llwyd Blaenau, ac
ef hefyd oedd perchen Gregynog (Hall) yn ôl yr achau Saesneg (gw.
M.C., iv, 384; L.D., i, 283, 284, 299; L.G.C., 431; M.C., ix, 306, 309,
311). Dyna'n fyr fy nadl dros Grugunog fel hen ffurf Gregynog.

Pam ynteu na phrintiais yr enw fel *Grugunog* yn y Sallwyr? Am y
rheswm fy mod wedi cael y ffurf *Gregynog* ar arfer er 1521, ac y mae 400
mlynedd yn rhoi peth awdurdod i enw. Os ydys am arfer hen ffurfiau
enwau lleoedd, rhaid adfer *Caer Dyf* am Gaerdydd, ac *Abertawy* am
Abertawe, *Llanddinan* am Landinam. A oes raid adfer *Aberhodni* am
Aberhonddu? Beth am droi Abermaw yn *Abermawdd?* Beth am *Aber
Seint* am Gaernarfon? Dyma ffordd na cherddaf hi o'm bodd. Derbyniwn
Caerdydd, nid am ei fod mor hynafol â *Chaerdyf*, ond am ei fod yntau
hefyd yn ddatblygiad naturiol yn Gymraeg, ac wedi ymgartrefu bellach.
Felly am y lleill.

Hoffwn olrhain hanes yr enw Grugunog yn fanylach, gan fod agwedd
gyffredinol ar y pwnc. Ond y mae damcanu yn ansicrach gorchwyl na
chasglu ffeithiau, ac yn llawer llai buddiol.

Y mae dau ddosbarth mawr o enwau lleoedd yn *-og, -iog*. Yn y cyntaf
ceir enwau a ffurfiwyd drwy roi *-iog* ar ôl enw person (perchen, sant),
megis *Brychan, Brycheiniog; Tudwal, Tudweiliog (Peulin, Peuliniog?); Cathen,
Catheiniog; Annhun, Annun, Anhuniog*, a llu o hen enwau godidog o'r fath.
Methaf gofio enghraifft yn *-og*, oddieithr ffurfiau fel *Catheinog*, lle collwyd
yr *i*. Rhaid tybio iddi fod yno i gyfrif am newid *e* yn *Cathen* i *ei*; felly
hefyd *Brycheinawc*.

Yn yr ail, rhoddwyd *-og* ar ôl enw peth i ddangos ei fod yn aml yn y
lle hwnnw, megis *mawn, mawnog; celyn, celynnog, clynnog; Brwyn, brwynog;
graean-og, calch-og, ceirch-iog, defeid-iog, eithin-og, maes-og, rhedyn-og*, etc. Ceir
-iog yn y rhain ar ôl *-ei-*, ond ni throir *a* yn *ei* o flaen y terfyniad cyffredin.
Pe rhoid y terfyniad *-og* ar ôl *Brychan*, ceid *Brychanog*, ond cf. *calchog*.

Weithiau amwys yw ffurf, e.e., ceir *Eithin* fel enw dyn yn L.L. 397
(tair enghraifft). Beth felly yw *Eithinauc* yn *Tref eithinauc*, td. 126? Ceir

Grucauc yn enw dyn, td. 240: ond rywsut gwell fuasai gennyf esbonio Llannerch-*rugog* fel llecyn â grug arno nac fel llannerch gŵr o'r enw hwn; eto cf. Llannerch *Hudol*, lle saif *hudol* am swynwr. Os -*iog* sydd amlaf o ddigon, onid yn gwbl, mewn enwau lleoedd o'r dosbarth cyntaf, gall hynny setlo bod Eithinog yn perthyn i'r ail. Eto ni ellir bod yn bendant: os yw Grugog yn enw personol, gall Eithinog fod hefyd. Aeth *Tre Walchmai* ym Môn yn bentref *Gwalchmai*: gallai *Tref Eithinog* yn gyffelyb roi *Eithinog* heddiw. Po fwyaf a gesglir o'r enwau hyn, anhawsaf yw eu dosbarthu.

I ddychwelyd at y pwnc. I ba ddosbarth y perthyn *Grugunog?* Haws ar hyn o bryd ei roi yn yr ail, oni cheir -*og* arall yn gwmni iddo yn y dosbarth cyntaf, neu oni cheir prawf mai enw dyn yw wedi dirywio yn enw lle, cf. *Gwalchmai* uchod.

Mewn Gwyddeleg ceir *fraoch*, 'heather,' a *Fraoch*, enw dyn; hefyd *Fraochan* (cf. *Bodrugan, Rec. Carn.*, 67). Ni welais *Grug* hyd yn hyn am ddyn yn Gymraeg, ond ceir *Grugyn* (B.A., 13, 9, Ysgwyt *rugyn* rac tarw *trin*) yn odli â *trin* (hefyd â *trun* yn yr un llinell, mewn orgraff hŷn, td. 34, 10, Scuyt *grugyn* irac taryf *trun*). Felly darllener fel *Grugin*, ond sylwer bod tuedd i gymysgu -*in*, ac -*yn* (*eurin, euryn; Myrddin, Myrddyn*). Yn bwysicach, gan fod yr hen *u* yn gron, gwneir y llafariad yn y sillaf nesaf yn grwn hefyd, a thry *i* yn *u*, cf. tal *rugun*, M.A., 163 (ystyr arall?). Dyna pam y ceir *Grucinan* yn hen orgraff Llyfr Llandaf, a *Grugunan* yng nghân Cynddelw; cf. hefyd *buddig*, a droes yn *buddug*; *buddigawl* yn *buddugawl*; felly *llurig*, ond *llurugeu, llurugawg* (gw. Skene, ii, 68, 73, 81; Gr. C., 116, 126; R.M., 113, 308, etc.): yn Llyfr Llandaf, 413, ceir hen ffurf Meurig, sef *Mouric*; cf. y rhestr o *Meuruc* yn y Mynegai, R.B.B., 437, yn -*uc*. Felly'n union y troai *Grucinauc* yn *Grugunauc*, a *Grugunog*, pe ffurfid enw o *Grugin*. Ochr yn ochr o ran ystyr, rhown *Grugin, Eithinin*, -*yn* (Sk., 74, 79, 96, 104), *Iscawin* (R.M., 108), *Iscawyn* (138); *Derwin* (yn *Bryn Derwin*); a'r sant bytholwyrdd a phigog (efallai) *Celynnin*. Am gymysgu -*in* ac -*yn*, nid mewn orgraff ond sain hefyd, gw. *gorllewyn* (D.N., 200). Hefyd cf. hanes *mebin* a'r tarddair *mabinogi*: pan ffurfiwyd *mebyn*, nid oedd ond cam i'r ffurf *mabynnogi*, y gair efallai sydd ynghudd yn y ffurf eithriadol *mabynnogyon* (P.K.M., xlii). Un *n* sydd yn meb*in*, dwy yn meb*ynn* (gw. W.G., 229); pe tybid i -*yn* ddisodli -*in* fel terfyniad *Grugyn*, cyfiawnheid rhoi *nn* yn *Gregynnog*.

Pan gollodd *u* ei chrynder tueddai i droi weithiau yn *e*, cf. *myned* am *mynud, munud* mewn rhai tafodieithoedd yn y De. Dyna'r unig ffordd y medraf esbonio *Gregyn* am *Grugyn* yn hanes hela'r Twrch Trwyth. Erlidiwyd *Grugyn* Gwrych Ereint i Geredigion, a lladdwyd ef, nid yn *Garth Grugyn* ond Garth *Gregyn*, medd y Llyfr Gwyn a'r Coch (R.M., 140, W.M., 503). Eto rhydd R.B.B., 369, gastell Garth*grugyn*, (gw. R.W.M., i, 724; ii, 848, yn Llanilar?) Onid yw hyn yn help i ddangos sut y trowyd *Grugunog* yn *Gregynog?*

Y mae'r Athro Gruffydd yn cyfeirio at *Y Rhedynnog*, ac *Yr Eithinog* gyda'r fannod, fel petai pob enw yn *-og* yn hawlio'r cyfryw. Ond cymysglyd iawn yw'r arfer hyd y gwelaf. Ni ches fannod o gwbl o flaen geiriau'r dosbarth cyntaf. Amrywia'r ardaloedd a'r llawysgrifau ynglŷn â'r ail. Ni chlywais erioed *Y Glynnog* yn Arfon, ac nid llygriad diweddar yw hyn chwaith. Yn *Hanes Gr. ap Cynan*, a ysgrifennwyd mewn rhan tua 1250, ceir (td. 114) 'a oedynt *yg kelynnawc;*' 118, '*yg kellynnauc vaur;*' 156, 'ar gymeint *y* Benmon, ar gymeint *y Gelynnavg* ar gymeint *y* Enlli' (lle saif *y* am 'i'); *Llyfr yr Ancr*, td. 124 (1346), y dref e hun a elwit *kellynnawc*; R.P., 94*a*, *is kelynnoc*, llawr *kelynnoc* vawr. Serch hynny, am y lle a elwir *Celynog*, ger Gregynog, ceir pobl o'r ardal mewn tystiolaeth gyfreithiol drosodd a throsodd yn ei alw '*the* Galynog,' neu '*the* Gelynog' (*Mont. Coll.*, ix, 312–3), er na ddywed yr un ohonynt '*the* Gregynog.' Yn M.A., 918, ceir *y ddyfynnoc*; ond, medd Lewys Glyn Cothi (td. 48), 'Ef â i Wynedd o *Ddyfynog.*' Yn R.W.M. i, 260, ceir *o'r Helygog*; 849, 'y plas yn *y gelchoc;*' 985, y *gyffyllioc*, ond ar yr un tudalen 'Rob. llwyd a gavodd *brynioc*,' a druan ohono, fe'i cafodd heb fannod. Nodais eisoes *Rhedynog Felen* heb fannod; ond cefais hefyd, R.M., 111, 'o dal y *redynawc du;*' W.M., 234*b*, 'o dal *y redynawc du*' (bannod, ond un *n*!). Yr unig reol a welaf yn hyn o beth yw arfer. Ac ni welaf reswm yn y byd dros wthio'r *y* i mewn lle nad yw arfer gwlad yn galw amdani.

Eithr nid cwestiwn o Gymraeg sydd yna yn unig, ond daw'r ieithoedd Celtig eraill i mewn, a'r Lladin hefyd. Gweler ysgrifau meithion d'Arbois yn y *Revue Celtique* (Cyf. viii a ix), ar enwau lleoedd yn *-iacus* (*-iog* yn Gymraeg) ac *-acus* (*-og*). Nid oes ofod nac amser i grynhoi ei drafodaeth, ond gellir dysgu llawer oddi wrthi am enwau lleoedd yng Nghymru. Gwahaniaetha rhwng y terfyniad *-iacus*, ac *-acus*; sylwa iddo gael 36 o enwau lleoedd lle ceid y cyntaf ar ôl enw dyn, a 9 yn unig o'r cyfryw yn diweddu gyda'r ail. Sôn y mae am Ffrainc (Gâl) yn ystod yr ymerodraeth Rufeinig (R.C., viii, 121); cf. uchod, *-iog*, ac *-og* yn y dosbarth cyntaf.

Dywed fod enwau lleoedd yn -acus gydag enw cyffredin yn fôn iddynt, i'w cael yn Llydaw o'r unfed ganrif ar ddeg; yr hynaf a welodd, meddai (td. 139), yw *Les Radenuc,* Llys Redynog (heb fannod, un *n*!). Dyry hefyd *Quelennec* a etyb i'n Celynnog ni, etc.

Ond gan mai prin yw'r enghreifftiau o roi *-og* ar ôl enw person i ffurfio enw lle yng Nghymru, gwell gofyn am esboniad arall. Cynigiaf fel ail bosibilrwydd fod *Grugunog* yn deillio o'r enw *grugin,* 'heather;' cf. *rhosin, gwernin* (Ll.A., 108, 110) a *hesgin, hesgyn.* Buasai *Grugunog* felly yn frawd neu chwaer i *Grugog!* Erys *tal rugun* Cynddelw hefyd i'w ystyried (M.A., 163).

Sut bynnag, ni rof bwys ar allu egluro'r tarddiad. Y peth a garwn ei gael fyddai enghreifftiau eto o gywyddau'r beirdd yn yr hen gyfnod a'r canol, i weld sut y defnyddient hwy yr enw. Y chwedl hwn a elwir y gainc gyntaf o rugunogi, eithr nid yma y mae terfyn arno. Pan ddaw chwaneg o oleuni, bydd raid ail agor y pwnc o'r cychwyn.

II

Nodiad gan y Golygydd

YR wyf yn gobeithio nad oes neb o ddarllenwyr y LLENOR yn dal yr hen gred Gymreig y dylai dyn 'ateb' pob beirniadaeth a dynno arno'i hunan. Pe buasai gennyf gymaint â throed iâr o dir danaf, buaswn yn myned ati i hel fy llyfrau ynghyd a cheisio llunio achos i wrth-brofi gosodiadau yr Athro Ifor Williams. Ond, hyd y gwn, ni bu erioed yn hanes ysgolheictod yng Nghymru well esiampl o un ochr yn profi'r pwnc yn derfynol nag ysgrif werthfawr yr Athro. Cyn rhoddi'r sachliain i guddio fy noethni a myned i'r twll lludw i gael rhywbeth ar fy mhen, dymunwn ddywedyd dau beth 'in mitigation of sentence,' chwedl y cyfreithwyr. Yn gyntaf, nid yw'r Athro'n hollol gywir wrth ddywedyd 'ceryddir fi' yn y frawddeg gyntaf. Dylaswn wrth gwrs fod wedi meddwl mai ef oedd yn gyfrifol am y coloffon, ond *ni* feddyliais hynny, a dyna'r gwir. Ac yn ail, y mae'n gryn linariad ar f'edifeirwch sylweddoli na buasai'r LLENOR na Chymru wedi cael yr ymdriniaeth orchestol a llafurfawr hon ar *Gregynog* oni bai i mi siarad cyn fy nhro; bûm felly yn offeryn annheilwng iawn i dynnu ffïolau gwybodaeth ddigymar yr athro am fy mhen. Os digwydd i mi wneuthur cyffelyb ffolineb eto, yr wyf yn gobeithio y bydd y gawod yr un mor dyner a chynhyrchfawr.

Dylaswn fod wedi bod yn ofalus gyda *Gregynog* yn anad un enw oherwydd, fel y gŵyr rhai o'r darllenwyr, yr wyf wedi bod yn galw sylw at eiriau 'perchenogol' fel *Ffestiniog*, ac wedi awgrymu y gall eraill fel *Ceiriog* ('tir Carus') fod yn eu plith. Yn wir, pan ddaeth y Llenor allan a phan ail ddarllenais yr adolygiad, rhuthrodd *Clynnog* yn ei holl noethni di-fannod i'm meddwl, ac o hynny hyd pan dderbyniais ateb yr Athro yr wyf wedi bod yn gwneud gwar amdani. Pan oeddwn i'n fachgen yn Arfon, sonnid am hogyn drwg yn 'magu cweir'; megais innau hi'n annwyl iawn, a thyfodd yn llafnes dan fy ngofal. Ac yn sicr, nid oes gennyf le i gwyno, dim ond rhyw led ddisgwyl y caf innau annhebyg gyfle rywdro i roddi cweir iddo yntau; os caf, yr wyf yn gobeithio y bydd mor drwyadl â hon.

THE NAME 'GREGYNOG'

MELVILLE RICHARDS

The Welsh literary quarterly *Y Llenor* first appeared in 1922, and continued without interruption for thirty years until 1951, firstly under the editorship of W. J. Gruffydd, then for the last six volumes under the joint editorship of Gruffydd and T. J. Morgan. *Y Llenor* was at first mainly distributed by the Welsh Societies of the four University Colleges, and students in the twenties and thirties will remember how eagerly we awaited each number: what did Gruffydd have to say this time in his salty editorial notes; what new poem, or article or short story, or essay would appear? The standard was consistently high, and could bear comparison with any other literary journal of its period. This must be said in order that the amicable dispute over the correct spelling of *Gregynog* may be put in its proper perspective.

Gruffydd had reviewed in the third number of Vol. IX (1930), *Psalmau Dafydd yn ôl William Morgan, 1588*, edited by Ifor Williams, Gwasg Gregynnog, 1929. He drew attention to the varying spellings in different volumes printed at the Press, i.e. *Gregynog*, 1925, 1926, 1927, *Y Gregynnog* 1928, *Gregynnog* 1929, and having wrongly assumed that Sir John Morris-Jones was responsible for 'correcting' the spelling to *Y Gregynnog*, he proceeded to complain that the definite article *y* was as necessary as in such forms as *Y Rhedynnog*, and that a case could be made against the double *-nn-*.

In the next number Ifor Williams (later Sir Ifor) replied to the complaint in a long note on the name, entitled characteristically simply *Gregynog* (with no definite article, and no *-nn-*). He chided Gruffydd for being so pedantic, and reminded him that it was he himself, Ifor Williams, not Sir John Morris-Jones, who was responsible for the form *Gregynnog* (without the definite article). Ifor Williams then proceeded to think aloud (this again was characteristic of his manner of working in which he would gently lead the reader through his own mental processes when he was discussing some thorny crux of etymology, or some new interpretation of a literary or historical conundrum). He began by noting that as so many Welsh place-names are found in a mutated form without the definite article, it would be natural to suppose that *Gregynog* was a mutated form of *Cregynog*. The Director of the Gregynog Press had asked him for his opinion on the form of the name, and he had found scores of examples of *Gregynog* without the article, and just one example of the double *-nn-*. He had also found the form *Grugunawc* (c. 1150). He therefore informed the Director that the definite article should be dropped, but that he was not absolutely sure about the *-n-* / *-nn-*, and therefore the name of the Press should be spelled *Gregynnog* until he could find more proof one way or the other. He confessed that in the intervening two years he now tended towards the single *-n-*, with a possible toleration of the double *-nn-*.

Ifor Williams then countered any possible criticism that Professors of Welsh were unable to decide whether there should be a single or double *-n-* in a Welsh word (it will be remembered that W. J. Gruffydd was Professor of Welsh at Cardiff, and Ifor Williams at Bangor!). He went on to answer Gruffydd's rash statement that *Y Rhedynnog* should be so spelled by showing that the correct etymological form is *Rhedynog*, without either article or double *-nn-*, except that by analogy with other names with an etymological double *-nn-*, one might find *Rhedynnog* at a later stage.

Then came the various forms of the name as evidenced in Welsh manuscript and documentary sources. The earliest is in a poem by Cynddelw (fl. 1150–1200):

> Grugunawc eryr grugunan gynnetyf
> 'the lord of Grugunawc (Mod. W. *Grugunog*) has the same qualities as Grugunan'.

The name Grugunan occurs elsewhere in an earlier spelling as *Grucinan*, i.e. a personal name *Grugin* or *Grugyn* with a suffix -*an*. *Grugunawc* probably refers to *Gregynog*, since Cynddelw was a poet of Powys. Later poets (up to the beginning of the sixteenth century) also have the form *Grugunog*, i.e. no article, and a single -*n*-. Why then did Ifor Williams not use this old form *Grugunog* in 1929 instead of *Gregynog*? The answer is that *Gregynog* came to be generally used during the sixteenth century, and it would be pedantically wrong to 'restore' the earlier form *Grugunog*, just as it would be wrong to use *Caerdyf* for 'Cardiff' instead of the current *Caerdydd*.

The discussion now turned to place names with the suffixes -*og*, -*iog*. The point was made that -*iog* is used as a suffix after a personal name, as in *Brycheiniog* ('land of Brychan'). -*og*, on the other hand, is used to denote frequency or abundance after a common noun, i.e. *mawn* 'peat', but *mawnog* 'turbary'; *calch* 'lime', but *calchog* 'abounding in lime'. If the common noun contains -*ei*- then the suffix becomes -*iog*, e.g. *ceirch* 'oats' and *ceirchiog* 'place abounding in oats'. (John Leland who made his famous itinerary in Wales in 1536–9 says of *Ceirchiog* in Anglesey, 'an otye place').

A place-name in -*og* may be ambiguous. *Eithin* ('gorse') occurs as a personal name: what then is the origin of the place-name *Eithinog*? It could be either 'a gorsy place' (from the common noun *eithin*), or it could be itself a personal name based on *Eithin*. How does one therefore explain *Grugunog*?

In Irish *fraoch* 'heather' is a common noun, and *Fraoch* is a personal name. The cognate Welsh *grug* 'heather' is a common noun, but there does not happen to be a personal name *Grug*. The name *Grugyn* does exist, however, but this raises another difficulty: -*in* and -*yn* are easily confused as suffixes in Welsh, added to which -*u*- in the first syllable can affect -*i*- in the following syllable and change it to -*u*-. This is why one has the two forms of the personal name *Grucinan* and *Grugunan*, just as the etymologically correct *buddig* 'victorious' (also as a personal name in Queen *Boudica*) became *buddug*. Thus the form *Gruginog* could become *Grugunog* if it were based on the name *Grugin*. Moreover, if *Grugin* and *Grugyn* were confused, then *Grugyn* + *og* could well become *Grugynnog*, *Gregynnog* with a double -*nn*-. Ifor Williams then went on to show that when Welsh -*u*- lost its rounded sound it could become -*e*- / -*y*- as in the South Walian form *myned* for *munud* 'minute'. Thus *Grugunog* could develop into *Gregynog*.

Now came the question of the definite article. Ifor Williams found great confusion in usage here, and quoted several examples of place-names in *-og* with and without the article. He came to the conclusion that as there was no example of *Y Grugunog* or *Y Gregynog*, there could be no point in insisting on the inclusion of the article in this particular case. He then went on to quote the usage in Celtic place-names in Gaul during the Roman occupation. Henry d'Arbois de Jubainville had distinguished between the suffixes *-iacus* (=Welsh *-iog*) and *-acus* (=Welsh *-og*), and had shown that the majority of examples of *-iacus* were added to a personal name. In Brittany, from the eleventh century on, the old *-acus* was found after a common noun. To clinch the argument Ifor Williams quoted the Breton *Les Radenuc* (=Welsh *Llys Redynog*), and underlined it by noting the absence of the definite article, and the presence of a single *-n-*.

In view of the rarity of *-og* as a place-name suffix after a personal name in Welsh, Ifor Williams then considered a second possibility, namely that *Grugunog* was a derivative of the common noun *grugin* 'heather'. He ended by hoping to find further examples of the name in the earlier poetry so as to establish the usage. The whole question would have to be re-opened in the light of further evidence.

Gruffydd ended the article with a graceful and humorous apology. He confessed that he had not realized that Ifor Williams was responsible for the form *Gregynnog* in the edition of *Psalmau Dafydd*. He also welcomed the correction of his error, without which the readers of *Y Llenor* would not have had the benefit of Ifor Williams's magisterial discussion of the name. He expressed the hope that he himself would be able to thrash Ifor Williams soundly on some future improbable occasion.

The discussion well illustrates the high standards of *Y Llenor*. It also brings into relief the friendly baiting of one professor by another. Thirdly, it shows how difficult it can be to find a complete and satisfactory answer to a particular onomastic problem, even though in the majority of cases the answer may be definitive. I might be allowed perhaps to add that *l'affaire Gregynog* is not quite the rarified 'academic' matter that it might seem to be at first sight, in view of the efforts now being made to establish acceptably correct forms for Welsh place-names.

Those sixteenth century poets who sang the praises of the Blaenau family of Gregynog were themselves very uncertain of the form of the name. I am indebted to Miss Enid Pierce Roberts for the following references.

Huw Arwystl in his elegy on Ieuan Llwyd ap Tomos has:
　　　trvan i bv vwch trwyn Bank
　　　troia am ektor ievank
　　　doir vn rryw drveni rrawc
　　　akw ar genedl Krvgvnawc
(where the *cynghanedd* proves *Crugunog*)

Lewys Dwn in a poem to Dafydd Llwyd has:
　　　Mam y glod hynod yw honn
　　　yn rroi gwin yn rregynnon
　　　yng rūgvnog wraig annwyl
　　　mork a rodd ym er kerdd wyl
(here the form is *Grugunog*)

Hywel ap Syr Mathew to Dafydd Llwyd has:
　　　Karw doeth yn Kowiro dadl
　　　Krygynog Kowir gynadl
　　　(*Crugynog*)

Gruffudd Hafren to Lewys Blaenau 'o Regynog' has:
　　　Parl garw gwyn, perl Gregynog
　　　(*Gregynog*)

Owain Gwynedd to Dafydd Llwyd 'o Gregynog' has:
　　　Aelwyd gron y wlad â'i gwres
　　　Yw Cregynog, caer gynnes
　　　(*Cregynog*)

　　　Caer deg iawn, caredig oedd
　　　Cregynog, lle ceir gwinoedd
　　　(*Cregynog*)

Siôn Mawddwy in an elegy to Lewys Blaenau:
　　　Duodd holl wlad Cydewen
　　　Dwyn Efrog Gregynnog wen
(*Gregynnog*, or possibly *Cregynnog*).

The *cywyddwyr* cannot always be relied on, simply because they frequently aired their own 'antiquarian' views. Later documentary forms are:

1615   Gregynoge (*British Records Association*)

1656   Cregynog otherwise Gregynog (Mtg. deeds at *Cardiff Free Library*)

1730   Greginnog (ditto)

1795   Gregynnog (*John Evans, Map of North Wales*)

1836   Gregynog (*Ordnance Survey*)

As for the personal name *Grugunan*, I can add a further example:

1247   Jorvert S. of Grugunnan (*Calendar of Charter Rolls*, iv. 460)

Unless 'filius' has been omitted, *Gruginan* is a place-name in the following:

1258   Iorwerth Gruginan (*Littere Wallie*, ed. J. Goronwy Edwards, 185).

I agree with Ifor Williams's conclusions almost in their entirety, and especially with his insistence on the authority of *usage*. I cannot, however, wholly accept the importance which he places on analogy: for instance he suggests that *Gregynog* could have become *Gregynnog* because there was a place-name *Celynnog* (with a double -*nn*-) nearby. The point here, I think, is the stress accent in a polysyllabic word or name where that stress accent falls on a syllable ending in -*n*. Usage is here conditioned by several factors; a good example may be found in the ancient territorial names like *Eifiònydd* and *Meiriònydd*. In both cases the -*n*- is etymologically a single -*n*-, but for one reason and another, *Eifionydd* has remained *Eifionydd*, while *Meirionydd* had become *Meirionnydd* by the fourteenth century at latest. However, it would take the sharpest of sharp-eared phoneticians to record the difference between *Eifionydd* and *Meirionnydd*. Welsh orthography is not altogether consistent (what orthographical system is?). *Brenin* 'king' is so spelled now even though we know that it comes from British **brigantinos*, a form which would give *breenhin* in medieval Welsh, and is so spelled in that period. In the plural *brenhìnoedd* we hear the original -*nt*- in the form -*nh*- before the accent. The trouble springs partly from the fact that in a monosyllabic word ending in a sonant *n, l, r*, the length of the preceding vowel varies according to the etymology of the word. This is why a circumflex accent is needed if the vowels *a, e, o, w, y* are long before *n, l, r*.

A single *n* in a polysyllabic word in Welsh almost forces one to believe that the preceding vowel is long. To write **brennin* in Modern Welsh would be a contradiction in terms simply because the -*e*- is long (it is in fact a contraction of *e-e* from the -*iga*- of **brigantīnos*), and even though an earlier -*nh*- in a disyllabic word should normally give -*nn*- in later Welsh.

In *Gregyn(n)og*, although most of us would hear a double -*nn*-, long orthographical usage has conditioned us to the *written* form *Gregynog*, and this will do no harm if it serves to remind us of the ancient and honourable name *Grugunog*.

CHAPTER THREE

THE BLAYNEY PERIOD

PRYS MORGAN

IN the volumes which make up the history of Brazil, Gilberto Freyre portrays his country's story not with dynasties or governments but with dwellings, now the colonial estate mansion, now the hut of the slaves. The same process of taking dwellings as symbols might be adapted for the story of Wales for at least one period, that of the *plas*, the little manor house of the gentry from the fifteenth to the eighteenth centuries. Gregynog was such a house. The Blayneys who lived there for the longest period in its long history were such a family. When historians use the word 'interesting' to describe a house or a family the word has two meanings. The Sudeley family or the Davies family who lived in more recent times at Gregynog were interesting in the sense of extra-ordinary. The Blayneys are interesting because of the other meaning for historians, interesting because they were utterly typical of their age and their class. In the microcosm of Gregynog we see mirrored the greater world of gentry Wales.

The name Blayney is curious and strange, and yet a symbol of the world in which the family rose to prominence. It is first recorded in a roll, the purpose of which is unknown, of burgesses of Welshpool in 1406—'Evan Blayney of Tregynon'.[1] He was known to his kinsmen in the hills west of Welshpool as Ieuan ap Gruffydd ap Llywelyn Fychan ap Llywelyn ab Einion ap Llywelyn ap Meilir Gryg. Those forefathers in his patronymic catalogue had lived at the farm of Llwyn Melyn in the northern part of Tregynon parish presumably since the twelfth century. The year 1406 was in the middle of the revolt of Owain Glyndŵr, and Ieuan may have felt it prudent to anglicise his name in the colonial atmosphere of the little town sheltering beneath the red walls of Powis castle. He lived in a marcher lordship—Ceri and Cedewain lay as twin lordships astride the Severn—and this was a colonial unit at this period, with descendants

---

[1] W. V. Lloyd, 'Early charters of Welshpool', *Montgomeryshire Collections,* xii (1878), 309–14, 320–56, esp. 313. M. C. Jones, 'The Feudal Barons of Powys', ibid., i (1866), 257 et seq. esp. 302.

of conquerors living in great castles such as Powis, with colonists filling the minuscule towns, while all around in the hill country like Tregynon there coexisted the native subjects, among whom were native gentry like Ieuan. His family memorised in defeat their ancient genealogies, which showed their forefather Meilir Gryg as a descendant of the Welsh lord of Cegidfa (Guilsfield) Brochwel ab Aeddan, and that he in turn was descended, albeit through illegitimate lines, from Brochwel Ysgithrog ancient king of part of Powys. The bards reminded each generation of its royal origins and its long history, indeed they showed each gentry family of the hills how it was akin one to another. Through Brochwel the Blayneys were akin to nearly every native family of note in Powys. Through their marriage with a daughter of Nannau they were related to nearly every family of note in Gwynedd. In this frontier world of the marches colonists might go native: the bard of Newtown, Hywel Swrdwal was of the De Surdevals, just as the later Tess was of the D'Urbervilles; and natives like Ieuan ap Gruffydd of Tregynon might take on the habits of the conquerors. His official surname Blayney may have been in origin a mere nickname: it refers clearly to his home in the *Blaenau*, the head-waters of the streams Rhiw and Bechan which flow about Llwyn Melyn and Gregynog. It would have mattered little to him that it was a nickname, but clearly the descendants long remained in doubt about their surname, since they occasionally added Lloyd to the Blayney, and some lines, such as the branch at Aberbechan or the lines at Manafon and Chirbury took the name Price from later members called 'Rhys' among Ieuan's de-scendants.[2] On the burgess roll of Welshpool in 1406 there also appears the unanglicized burgess Gruffydd Fychan ap Gruffydd Deuddwr, the ancestor of the Weaver family of Betws Cedewain, whose fortunes later became so intertwined with those of the Blayneys, and who were the ancestors of the Sudeley family. Blayney then is an unusual kind of Welsh surname, a geographical one of a kind common in England but very rare in Wales—a similar one from the same area would be Kyffin (from Cyffin meaning a border as in Cyffin in the parish of Llangadfan). It is

---

[2] N.L.W. Peniarth MS. 132, ff. 23–4 'Descendants of Ieuan Blaene'. S. R. Meyrick (ed.), *Heraldic visitations of Wales by Lewys Dwnn,* (Llandovery 1846), i, 284, 288, 298, 299. Ibid. i, 312 has the best printed version of the list of Welshpool burgesses mentioned in note 1 *supra,* a list of which the purpose is unknown, for the men on it were probably supporters of Owain Glyndŵr. W. V. Lloyd, *The Sheriffs of Montgomeryshire* (London 1876), pp. 137, 139–40, 141–2, 145–7, 186, 188–9, 227, 238–9, 495, 507. E. Rowley-Morris 'The Family of Blayney', *Mont. Colls.* xxi (1887), 273–302. A good MS Blayney genealogy, composed around 1667, is in N.L.W. Bronwydd MS. 2, f. 20.

a Welsh word, but turned into a surname of an English type, and seems to be symbolic of the marcher world.

Ieuan, or Evan Blayney, was a Welsh gentleman seeking minor office in a small marcher lordship. His ancestors had apparently lived for at least seven generations at Llwyn Melyn in Tregynon, the first being Meilir Gryg who may have lived in the late twelfth century. This is near the period when we first see the name of Gregynog recorded, in a poem by the royal poet of the court of Powys, Cynddelw Brydydd Mawr (*fl.* 1150–1200) who mentions in an elegy to the otherwise unrecorded sons of Dwywc fab Iorwerth 'Grugunawc eryr Grugunan gynnetyf ("Eagle of Gregynog, inborn nature of Grugunan")'.[3] This Dwywc had no connexion with any known ancestors of the Blayney line. The status of the Blayneys can be seen by the houses into which they married at this early date, Mathafarn near Machynlleth, Nannau in Llanfachreth, houses of the greatest standing. Evan himself married Elen Lloyd of Mathafarn, an aunt of the poet, prophet and gentleman Dafydd Llwyd on whose prophecies Henry Tudor was to set such store in 1485. The ode to the three sons of Evan Blayney beginning 'Trindod sy'n troi o undyn' has been attributed to Dafydd Llwyd, but it seems just as likely that it is by Ieuan son of Hywel Swrdwal, the bard who was a neighbouring burgess in Newtown, and a bard remarkable for having written an 'awdl' in the strict metres, but in Medieval *English*. It was indeed a frontier society.[4] The three sons were Howel, from whom descended the lines in the northern part of the patrimony towards Manafon in the Rhiw valley, such as Price of Manafon and Blayney of Stingwern (between Llanfair Caereinion and Llanerfyl); secondly Owen, who founded a family at Aberbechan, where Bechan flows into Severn near Newtown, and who climbed to the office of deputy steward of Richard Duke of York in the marcher lordship of Cedewain, and who later became an esquire of the body to the duke's son, King Edward IV; the third son Griffith lived at Gregynog, and became the ancestor of the line of Blayneys who made the name most famous. Evan's daughter Efa married

---

[3] J. Morris-Jones and T. H. Parry-Williams (eds.), *Llawysgrif Hendregadredd* (Caerdydd 1933), f. 68b. line 5.

[4] E. Pierce Roberts, *Braslun o Hanes Llên Powys* (Dinbych 1965), p. 97. Islwyn Jones, *Gwaith Hywel Cilan* (Caerdydd 1963), pp. xxi-ii, for attributions of the *cywydd* to the sons of Ieuan Blaenau. It is attributed to Hywel Cilan in N.L.W. Llanstephan MS. 53, f. 77. T. Tegwyn Jones, 'Gwaith Edward Urien a Gruffudd Hafren', (N.L.W. University of Wales M.A. thesis 1966); J. Afan Jones, 'Gweithiau Barddonol Huw Arwystl', (N.L.W. University of Wales M.A. thesis 1926); Roy Saer, 'Gwaith Owain Gwynedd' (N.L.W. University of Wales M.A. thesis 1961).

Dafydd Ddu, whose surname was to be made most famous by their great-grandson Dr. John Dee, the Elizabethan magus.

Like many of the Welsh native gentry during the so-called Wars of the Roses they were Yorkists. A bard who was one of the finest ever seen in Wales, and who sang many poems to Lancastrian and Yorkist gentry was Lewys Glyn Cothi, and he has left us a beautiful ode to the two brothers Owen of Aberbechan and Gruffydd of Gregynog.[5] The two brothers are 'swans as white as a water lily from Tregynon yonder', and the bard showers compliment after compliment upon them, showing what essential supports they were for the life of the countryside, and that they were men for whom the bard would do anything—'I would go to these two men of my language . . . through endless fires, through waves of the sea'. But the bard is like 'an archer with his white arrow', shooting between two targets, the two being the *plasau* or halls of the brothers, which he says he will visit as long as he has strength in him. On these visits he is sure to be lavishly entertained—'Were I older than the aged eagle, I should have this in these men's houses: white flour like the flour of Gwynedd, meat, Shrewsbury ale and mead, songs on all the subjects of the wide world, memory of the roots, through storytelling, I would hear every word of three languages, I would hear at my end two languages, and I would see steeds like seagulls with their men astride them'. One assumes that the 'three languages' were English, Welsh and maybe French, while the two languages to end his life would be Welsh and Latin. This magnificent paean of praise, all done in the alliterative metres of the traditional *cywydd*, ends with a reference to two other brothers, Romulus and Remus who founded the city of Rome, two whom the bard likens to his 'two hawks of Cedewain', to whom he now wishes long life.

Such a poem need not, indeed cannot, be taken literally, it is a beautifully turned courtly compliment by one of the best bards of the golden age of Welsh bardistry. It shows that the status of the family was indeed high by the mid-fifteenth century. Poems in a similar vein were written to the Blayneys, and to families in a cycle of small *plasau* in the area, right up to the mid-seventeenth century. Some give praise for the wine and lavish welcome of Gregynog (*gwin*, for wine, easily harmonises in Welsh alliterative verse with the central syllable of Gregynog), some are solemn

---

[5] J. Jones (ed.), *Poetical Works of Lewis Glyn Cothi* (London 1839–40), ii, 431–3.

and stately elegies for the death of the head of the house, and others seem to have little purpose other than to recall to each generation the long genealogies, in male and female lines, of the family. In these more or less tribal incantations one constantly hears reiterated the descent from Brochwel Ysgithrog (whose 'three nags heads erased' became the heraldic bearings of the Blayneys of Gregynog), or more recently the names of Gwyn and Gwennwys sons of Gruffydd ap Beli lord of Cegidfa (Guilsfield) Broniarth and Deuddwr. No poems by the Blayneys themselves survive, but their close kinsman by marriage Dafydd Llwyd of Mathafarn was famous for his vaticinatory or historical-political poetry, and Dafydd Llwyd of Dolobran (whose surname was later made world-famous in English banking) was a squire and a bard in the locality, while in the reigns of Elizabeth I and the early Stuarts, Lewys and James Dwnn, of Glanbechan in Betws Cedewain were squires and rhyming genealogists, poets a far cry from their kinsman and contemporary in England, John Donne.

The accession of Henry Tudor, head of the Lancastrian branch of the royal family, in 1485 did not appear to change the fortunes of the Blayneys, any more than it proved a setback for other great Welsh Yorkist families like the Herberts. The son of Griffith Blayney of Gregynog was Evan Lloyd Blayney, whose mother was the heiress of the house of Maesmawr near Caersws, and who became a squire to Henry VII, steward of the lordships of Ceri, Cedewain, Arwystli and Cyfeiliog, and constable of Montgomery castle.[6] He presumably adopted the extra surname Lloyd from his mother's family of Mathafarn, and the name continued to be used for the next three generations at Gregynog. Evan Lloyd's wife was Catherine the daughter of a small landowning family at Newtown, her grandfather Rhys ab Dafydd Llwyd having been killed in 1469 at the battle of Banbury with the flower of the Welsh gentry, and having earned an elegy from the bard of Mathafarn, yet another Dafydd Llwyd.[7] Like the Blayneys a few years later this family added to its property by leasing the abbey lands of Strata Florida. The Blayneys in the early years of the sixteenth century came into contact with the great clan of the Herberts: Sir Richard Herbert became receiver of Cedewain in 1514, and we find a few years after this that Evan's son Thomas ab Evan Lloyd Blayney

---

[6] W. Scott Owen, 'Parochial History of Tregynon', *Mont. Colls.*, xxx (1896), 1–168, esp. 61–2.
[7] W. Leslie Richards, *Gwaith Dafydd Llwyd o Fathafarn* (Caerdydd 1964), pp. 125–7.

made two marriages into the Herbert clan, a first marriage to Gwenllian Herle, and a second to Margaret Herbert of Montgomery, Thomas Herle and Richard Herbert being half-brothers. This was a dynastic contact of great importance, and the Blayneys of Gregynog were well poised to take advantage of the great changes to civil government of the English type coming over the marcher lordships after the acts of Union 1536 and 1542, and to make some profit from the Reformation. It is likely that the Blayneys had leased monastic lands for generations: in 1521, some years before the Henrician reformation, for instance, Celynog, a grange of Strata Florida, was leased by Gruffudd ab Howel ab Ieuan Blayney, a grange which eventually fell into the hands of the Gregynog line in 1577.[8] In 1543–4 Thomas ab Evan Blayney of Gregynog bought the reversion of the rectory of Betws from his cousin Rees Wyn ap Gruffudd ab Howel.[9] Thomas was a member of the Grand Jury of the new county of Montgomery in Henry VIII's reign, and one or two documents survive in his archive to show that he fairly aggressively tried to build up the family lands in the area. In 1550–1 we find that Thomas enfeoffed his son David Lloyd Blayney for the property of Gregynog,[10] and this may have been a device for avoiding feudal dues or death duties. Thomas probably went to live at his grandmother's property of Maesmawr near Caersws. There still remains at Maesmawr a magnificent black and white Tudor house, though it probably dates from rather later than Thomas's time. While his heirs from his marriage with Gwenllian Herle lived at Gregynog, his heirs from Margaret Herbert established a line at Maesmawr, and they possibly built the beautiful house which survives today.

The acts of Union had introduced into the marcher areas the English county system with its J.P.s and its high sheriffs, and unlike so many feudal and marcher offices, these were filled by descendants of native gentry. The family of Aberbechan, a line senior to Gregynog, though not as senior as those of Manafon and Stingwern, reached the office of high sheriff in the person of Rhys ab Morus in 1565, after whom the family decided to take the name Price. David Lloyd Blayney did not reach the same office till 1577, with his son Lewis as under-sheriff. David's father-in-law, possibly to be identified with Lewis Jones or Lewis Gwyn, high

---

[8] Gloucester Record Office, Sudeley MSS. MSS. 8, 72, 974, 975.
[9] Sudeley MSS. 79, 80. Rees Wyn was the head of the most senior line of the descendants of Ieuan Blaenau.
[10] Lord Sudeley, 'Gregynog before the Year 1900', *Mont. Colls.*, lxii (1971), 167–8.

sheriff in 1543 and 1558, was constable of Bishop's Castle, just over the border, and both he and David Lloyd Blayney seem to have patronised a number of bards such as Owain Gwynedd, Bedo Hafesb, Lewys Dwnn, Hywel ap Syr Mathew, and Huw Arwystl. New offices and old praises— this is not so much modern Wales, it should be remembered, as *early* modern Wales.

The bard Owain Gwynedd sang many poems to the members and kinsmen of the great family of Mathafarn near Machynlleth, in the latter half of the sixteenth century. Two poems by this bard survive to 'Dafydd Llwyd Blaenau'. The first begins by relating his ancestry with dignity, not only the tribe of Brochwel, but also his Herle ancestors in West Wales, back to the medieval lords of Tywyn near Cardigan, who were so famous for their patronage of the bards. After praising Tregynon, he turns to 'the very fair fortress, which was so generous, where one gets wine, a right royal court where a poor creature may always find generosity from the hand of fair Elisabeth'. Elisabeth Jones or Gwyn was Blayney's first wife. The second poem is rather more important: it apostrophises him as 'Blaenor holl waed Blaenau' (chief of the race of Blayney), and rehearses all his genealogy in a most random and roundabout way with the twining intricacy of an ancient Celtic interlacing carved on stone. Then it turns to Gregynog itself 'round hearth of the country, its warmth is Gregynog, warm fortress, where nine armies can be, with bards and men and tables with wine; there is beer for us for our feast, and thither will I go for a holiday! . . . Behold the house with the merry door, full of goodness, a grove of men!' It then refers to Blayney's office as sheriff, which the bard saw as an office of peacemaking after misgovernment, or misrule and which this time would be to the profit of the county.[11] Another poem of 1577, by Lewys Dwnn refers to David's wife as Eva Lloyd or Efa Llwyd of Eglwyseg, and refers to David's having built at Gregynog 'a fair new hall-house',[12] which possibly dates the main structure of the old Gregynog which survived up to the early nineteenth century.

David Lloyd Blayney died in 1595 and his eldest son Lewis did not long survive him, but died in 1601 leaving a ten-year-old boy John as heir. John was named after his maternal grandfather Sir John Price of

[11] Roy Saer, op. cit., *Cywyddau* 49, 52, on pp. 163, 172.
[12] N.L.W. Peniarth MS. 96, f. 614 'Neuadd-dŷ newydd-deg' in the original Welsh.

Newtown, one of the most important gentlemen in the county, and ancestor of the Pryce baronets of Newtown Hall. One of the last Welsh poems in praise of the Blayneys of Gregynog was a long funeral ode to Lewis Blayney written around 1601 by Edward Urien. It is the kind of solemn and closely-woven elegiac piece which would have been immediately comprehensible to any Welsh chieftain of the previous thousand years, but sadly incomprehensible to any of the successors of Lewis Blayney. It referred to the abject sorrow of Britain, mourning the death of the 'pearl of Gregynog', and having related Lewis's virtues it greeted the new heir 'Sion Blaenau', the 'golden-featured John of the weighty reason, or John whom two countries now adore, John heir of fortune, sense and party, let him stand and be honoured, with fame, for his father with the language of fair angels, has gone to the light. But woe to all Tregynon, for its anguished cold loss!'[13]

It might have been an elegy for the Welsh language at Gregynog itself. No poems actually to members of the family of Gregynog are known after this date, although Edward Urien, and the genealogist poets like James Dwnn go on singing the praises of the lesser gentry of the area till the middle of the century. The lesser gentry apparently went after 1660 into a sharp decline in wealth and status which left them with few means or desires to continue the old system of bardic patronage which had had an Indian Summer, as it were, in the reign of Elizabeth.

John Blayney, 'John of the weighty reason' to Edward Urien, inherited Gregynog as a child and lived for nearly three-quarters of a century there, became a barrister in the Inner Temple in 1609, became high sheriff of the county in 1630 and 1643, and in 1632–3 became steward of the lordships of Ceri, Cedewain and Halcetor and Montgomery, on behalf of the Herbert family, who by this time were dominating the county from their recently-purchased Powis Castle. The more senior kinsmen, the Prices of Aberbechan, had faded from importance by this time, for their heiress had married the heir of the great Cardiganshire house of Gogerddan (now the University College's Plant Breeding Station). The other branches spread in number—into Herefordshire, for example, even during the sixteenth century—but declined in importance. Owen Blayney of Stingwern (the senior branch) sold Pwllan to John Blayney in 1626, rented Dol y Vachwen to him in 1627, and sold him

13 Tegwyn Jones, op. cit. p. 44.

Bryncamisir in 1628.[14] It appears that a number of the branches of the Blayneys were in some considerable monetary difficulties and had to sell or mortgage their properties to their more successful kinsmen during the century. With his legal education, and his public offices under the Herberts, John Blayney was in a good position to strengthen his estate: in 1639, for example, he took a lease of the forest of Tregynon (presumably all the wild parts and commons of the area) from the Herberts of Powis.[15] A neighbour of somewhat more humble origins, Arthur Weaver of Highgate, Betws Cedewain, also became a lawyer in London, and rapidly built up an estate in Betws Cedewain, and at Morville, near Bridgnorth (he married the Smith heiress of that house), an estate whose fortunes were to become in this period closely interwoven with those of Gregynog.[16]

The wealth and social status of John Blayney appear to make it quite possible that the house we have illustrated in the eighteenth century water-colour by Pennant's collaborator Moses Griffith was extended from his grandfather's structure in the early seventeenth century by him, for this gabled many-chimneyed three-storeyed brick mansion in the picture has a distinctly Jacobean air; a further piece of testimony to his grand pretensions is the still surviving carved parlour at Gregynog, dated 1636. John had married Elizabeth Lloyd of Berthlwyd near Llanidloes, daughter of a family whose praises were still sung most fulsomely by many Welsh bards. But the lavish heraldic emblazoning in the carved parlour betokens a new age, when heraldry was replacing the more traditional Welsh delight in *achau a barddas,* genealogy and bardistry. Most of the arms displayed are those of semi-legendary Welsh chieftains or princes, the three nags heads of Brochwel Ysgithrog, the three cocks of Einion Sais, the lion rampant of Cynwrig ap Rhiwallon, the fleurs-de-lys of Collwyn ap Tangno, the spearheads of Caradog Freichfras, the three eagles of Owain Gwynedd, the wolf of Bleddyn ap Maenarch, the red hand in the dragon's mouth of Rhys Goch or of Phylip Hir, all these

---

[14] For many lesser branches of the Blayneys, see R. H. Blayney 'On Tracing a Pedigree', *Mont. Colls.,* lvii (1961–2), 42–9, and 'Catalogue of some Blayney wills', ibid., 46–7. Also S. P. Thomas, 'Wanderings of a royal tribe', ibid., lvi (1960), 114–24. For the sales of farms to John Blayney, see Sudeley MSS. 161, 166, 173.

[15] Sudeley MS. 233.

[16] E. Lhuyd, *Parochialia* (London 1911), iii, 71 mentions Mr. Weaver's house at Highgate, in its description of 'Bettus'. Weaver's pedigree made up by Lewis Dwnn (but never included in the 1846 edition) is preserved in the Sudeley MS. 959. The MS. is in box Q2 at Gloucester Record Office, and it appears to have been brought up to date in 1747 by the last of the Weavers of Betws and Morville. Morville was long the home of the Actons, and now belongs to the National Trust. There are innumerable references in Sudeley MSS to Arthur Weaver.

were the armorial bearings of the Welsh ancestors or kinsmen of the Blayneys who like all the Welsh native gentry claimed descent from the branches of the Welsh royal tribes. A few of the bearings of the carved parlour refer to recent marriages, the wheatsheaf badge probably was of the Herle family, the three lioncels were those of the Herberts (to whom both John Blayney and his wife were related), and lastly, like a joker in the pack, we see the strange coat of the trefoils belonging to the Loftus family. This records the marriage of John's only daughter and heiress Joyce, to her cousin Arthur Blayney, whose mother was the daughter of Archbishop Loftus of Dublin. This introduces us to another facet of the history of the Blayneys.

John Blayney's father Lewis, who died in 1601, had probably fought for many years as a professional soldier for Queen Elizabeth, together with his two brothers Thomas and Edward, first of all in the Low countries, then moving to Ireland in 1599 with Robert Devereux the ill-fated Earl of Essex. Edward the youngest brother was a most remarkable man, who rose to great prominence in the Elizabethan and Jacobean conquest of Ireland, and was raised to the Irish peerage as Lord Blayney. His particular care was the conquest and colonisation of what is today the county of Monaghan, and his colonial fortress was near Lough Mucknoe, and was called Castle Blayney, a name it retains to this day. He peopled the colony with many Welsh families, some of them, such as the Owen or Blayney-Owen family of New Grove, Monaghan, being kinsmen. Robert Blayney, M.P. for Monaghan in the Dublin parliament, was a cousin, born in Wales. In the Irish rebellion of 1641 the Blayneys suffered terribly, and some like the second Lord Blayney were killed, but the family survived, kept up very close contact with their cousins in Gregynog until the early eighteenth century, and produced a line of Lords Blayney lasting down to the decline of the estate and the extinction of the title in the later nineteenth century. For some unaccountable reason the Irish branch took up the name Cadwallader in the eighteenth and nineteenth centuries, and one of the lords of this name was a daring and successful commander of British troops in many parts of the world such as South Africa during the Napoleonic wars. Although the title is extinct, there are many families in Ireland bearing the surname Blayney, some of considerable importance in modern Irish history, and these are probably descendants of some cadet branches.

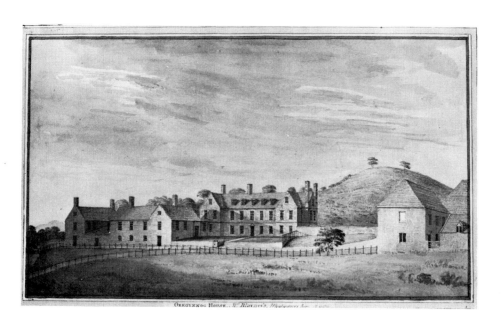

GREGYNOG IN THE LATER EIGHTEENTH CENTURY,
WATERCOLOUR BY MOSES GRIFFITH

The younger grandson of the first Lord Blayney, Arthur, came back to Wales and married his cousin Joyce the heiress of Gregynog and apparently lived with his parents-in-law at the hall. We find Arthur Blayney (who had lived at Castle Shane in Monaghan before his marriage) buying up property around Tregynon in 1637, but before he had long settled down, the family was shaken by the political upheavals of the 1640s which led to the civil wars. Blayney played a part of considerable importance in these wars. Like most of the Welsh gentry the Blayneys were royalists, and suffered (according to their family tomb at Tregynon parish church) much in the service of the 'royal martyr'. Arthur, who distinguished himself in the battle of Beaumaris in 1648 as a royalist commander, had in 1647 taken part under William Owen of Brogyntyn in the seige of that final bastion for Charles I, Harlech Castle. Charles I on 21 September 1645 is said to have passed Gregynog on his way from Newtown to Llanfyllin on one of his recruiting drives in Wales, but there is no record that he stopped there.[17]

It is rather difficult to find out what exactly happened to the Blayneys during the civil wars; they are not specifically mentioned in the royalist composition papers. Their friend and neighbour Arthur Weaver of Betws is mentioned more than once, clearly he wandered about much during the civil wars, appears to have been forced to fight on both sides, claimed to have lost as much as £3,000 from the despoliation of his fine estate around Bridgnorth, and his property was subjected to searching enquiry. Weaver clearly surrendered to the Roundheads in 1645 and took the loyal oath to the National Covenant in 1646. He appears to have been forgiven and to have been free to resume his business after this. The Blayneys of Gregynog were accused in 1652 of being 'papists and fathers of papists', and yet were forgiven as being no delinquents and excused by the county sub-committee.[18] There is thus no evidence that they paid any heavy fines to Parliament for their royalism. Arthur Blayney, who had been knighted by Charles I for his valiant service in battle, died in 1659. When Charles II was restored in 1660 he considered setting up a new order of chivalry, paying particular honour to those gentlemen who

---

[17] E. Rowley-Morris, 'The Family of Blayney', art. cit., *Mont. Colls.,* xxi (1887), 273–301, xxii (1888), 71–110, is the fullest treatment. See also A. H. Dodd, *Studies in Stuart Wales* (Cardiff 1952), pp. 81, 83.

[18] E. Rowley-Morris, art. cit., xxii, 78–9, J. R. Phillips, *The Civil War in Wales,* (London 1874), i. 380, ii, 269. G. Sandford, 'The Blayneys and Lords Sudeley', *Mont. Colls.,* xviii (1885), 229–44, and E. Rowley-Morris, 'Royalist Composition Papers', ibid., 71–9, 269–73.

had devoted themselves to his service, to be called the Order of the Royal Oak. John Blayney was nominated in extreme old age as one of these knights. There were to be some 75 of them from all the counties of Wales. The scheme was to cause such intense bitterness and re-crimination that Charles wisely dropped it. A survey of 1662 shows us that John's estate amounted to about £1,000 *per annum*, which made him one of the most substantial gentlemen in the county.[19]

John Blayney died in 1665, having outlived his son-in-law and daughter, and he was succeeded by his younger grandson Henry Blayney. The estate enters upon a period of 'mark-time' rather than progress, while the neighbouring estate of Arthur Weaver (who died in 1688) at Betws advanced rapidly in the later seventeenth century, both around Morville, within the town of Bridgnorth, and also around Betws Cedewain. When in 1667 Weaver became high sheriff, his undersheriff was one Thomas Blayney (possibly Blayney of Coedyperthi), and even though he owned the still surviving house of Highgate at Llaneithion, Betws, one of the Blayneys appears to have lived there. In the later years of the seventeenth century we do not find many farms added to the Gregynog estate, the estate on the contrary is frequently mortgaged, for example in 1670 to Humphrey Blunden of Worthen, Salop (a mortgage not entirely paid off even in the middle of the eighteenth century), and in 1674 to the Cornwall family of Ludlow and Berrington. In 1691 Henry Blayney mortgaged the estate for a further £1,250 in order to pay for the dowries of his many daughters.[20] These mortgages appear enormous, but they were still light compared with the true value of the estate. The gentry at this time were always short of cash, always living above their income, always borrowing, often from lawyerly families (the Weavers were such a family), and apparently always able to survive.[21]

Henry's many daughters, six out of the seven, were married off, but the only son John married in 1707 the well-endowed Ann Weaver of Betws, daughter of Arthur Weaver the younger, at last uniting in marriage the two neighbouring families. At this period 1710–13 the Weavers built the charity almshouses at Betws Cedewain, and apparently

---

[19] Sudeley MS. 1087, for evidence that John Blayney was appointed deputy to the Earl of Carbery for the county of Montgomeryshire in 1660. Blayney's estate rental for 1662 is Sudeley MS. 2153/AD/18.

[20] Sudeley MSS. 321, 343, and many other documents relating in one way or another to these many mortgagings in the later seventeenth century.

[21] For a general survey see H. J. Habakkuk, 'England', in A. Goodwin (ed.), *The European Nobility in the Eighteenth Century* (London 1967), 1–21.

Anthony Weaver lived at Penarth, the beautiful black and white farmhouse near Newtown. But the chief base of the Weavers in the eighteenth century was at Bridgnorth. In the early eighteenth century the Blayneys of Gregynog and the Weavers of Betws were blessed with numerous children. But by a curious trick of fate in both cases, few of the children either survived infancy or lived to marry or to produce heirs. The only surviving son of John and Ann Blayney was a bachelor, Arthur Blayney (1716–95), and the only surviving Weaver by the later eighteenth century was Susannah, daughter of the Anthony Weaver who had lived at Penarth, and who married Henry Tracy of Toddington, Gloucestershire, in 1767.[22] The Irish Lord Blayney probably learnt of the dire genealogical straits of the Blayney line, and the story goes (there is no evidence that the story is true) that Lord Blayney made what amounted to a state visit to the Blayneys at Gregynog, but Arthur Blayney and his unmarried sisters were much put out either by his pretentiousness or by the suggestion implied in the visit that they should make the Irish lords Blayney the heirs to the estate, and determined to have nothing to do with them. From the various wills of the Weaver brothers of the mid-eighteenth century it does appear that they all had most amicable relations with Blayney, made him their legatee and executor, perhaps knowing full well that ultimately Blayney would leave the whole estate to his cousin Susannah Weaver or her heirs. Her trustee was Arthur Blayney, and he received in instalments by various wills in 1759, 1761 and 1783, the great Weaver estates in England and in Montgomeryshire. By his own will in 1788 Blayney left his total estate, which was very considerable by Welsh standards, to Susannah's husband Henry Tracy, later Viscount Tracy of Toddington. This gradual intermarriage with English families and involvement with English estates was typical of many Welsh gentry families in the eighteenth century.

Arthur Blayney, last of the Blayney squires of Gregynog, has been in a way immortalised by a long pen-portrait of him in Philip Yorke of Erddig's edition of *The Royal Tribes of Wales*. Arthur Blayney was clearly

---

[22] The Sudeley MSS. for the eighteenth century period have innumerable references to the Weaver line, showing the elaborate family compacts made between the Weavers and the Blayneys. For the Tracy family, see Lord Sudeley, 'Toddington and the Tracys', *Transactions of the Bristol and Gloucestershire Archaeological Society*, lxxxviii (1969), 127–72; and ibid., M. J. McCarthy, 'Tracy of Toddington Manor', ibid. lxxxiv (1965), 161–74. The Irish Christian Brothers who own Toddington have placed recently at the Gloucester Record Office a collection of deeds, item 35 of which concerns Llandinam and Llanwnog and Penstrowed in the period 1628–1725.

a squire after Philip Yorke's own heart, a backwoods Welsh gentleman, frugal in his own habits, generous to others, maintaining his own wealth by improving the lot of his tenantry. The book of Philip Yorke consists of lists of descendants of the medieval chieftains of Wales, with Yorke's comments in lengthy footnotes upon the present day representatives of these medieval lines. 'Arthur Blayney . . . was descended from Brochwel Ysgithrog, a Prince of Powys, in the seventh century, but he valued himself on his pedigree no otherwise than by taking care that his conduct should not disgrace it.' He treated his tenants as friends, did all he could to help them improve their lands. He was generous and hospitable, his table appears to have been open to any traveller, 'he never indulged in far-sought delicacies, preferring the ducks and chickens of his poor neighbours, which he bought in all numbers, whether he wanted them or not.' He seems to have kept up the open handed hospitality for which Gregynog had been renowned in the time of his Tudor ancestors, though Yorke would put it differently from Owain Gwynedd 'it would be difficult to find another house where the visitor was more perfectly at his ease, from the titled tourist to the poor, benighted way-worn exciseman who knew not where else to turn'. His hounds were treated with perhaps a foolish generosity, for they were apparently so well fed and fat that they were of little use for hunting. He was apparently suspicious of lawyers, and of politicians, would not have anything to do with county or national politics, would not accept public office, although often pressed to do so (not unnaturally, since he was one of the great landowners of mid-Wales at a time when politics was run by landowners), and Yorke clinches this backwoods conservatism with the story that he always ordered a suit to be made for him in London, which by the later years of the eighteenth century must have been ridiculously old-fashioned, for he had not seen his tailor for forty years and he merely sent instructions that the new coat should be precisely like the last. Yorke also mentions that Blayney was well read and had a good library at Gregynog (we have no record of his books however), and that he visited Morville in Salop for part of the year and that his heirs the Tracys would visit him during the Summer for about a month in each year at Gregynog. He was certainly not a man for the London season. In a way this is an idyllic portrait of a generous and neighbourly country squire of the old school, where kindness and help meant far far more than money and profits and cash accounts, a quintessence of the virtues of the pre-industrial society. Yorke in other words has written a bardic *cywydd* in praise of Blayney, but in English prose.[23]

Blayney was in truth a figure a good deal more modern than the man portrayed by Philip Yorke. His memory was kept green for many generations among the local farmers and peasantry, according to people in the later nineteenth century, but this was partly because he had been a most active agrarian improver; willing to carry out new agricultural fashions and techniques, and if Townshend can be called 'Turnip Townshend' then at Gregynog we have 'Turnip Blayney'.[24] He rebuilt cottages and churches (for example the parish church of Tregynon), had a careful policy of conservation of stands of timber, always preferring to buy the timber of other landowners, and he invested in some early industrial projects, such as the sum of £3,000 in a canal. In 1791 he was lending money to Thomas Percy, Bishop of Dromore, an important figure in the literary history of England and of Wales, in order to help Percy's nephew at Bridgnorth. He actively built up the estate, and was busily buying properties right up to his death. He was not at all averse to new inventions: on 18 January 1795 (just before he died) we find him paying ten shillings to have four local children inoculated.[25] He did not live on a lavish scale, certainly, and the evidence of his accounts is that he bought great quantities of fish and game—salmon, perch, ravens, kite, rather than more expensive or exotic delicacies. His one extravagance seems to have been a constant supply of pipes of port, usually fifty pounds worth at a time, which would sometimes reach him via Shropshire from London, sometimes by ship from Liverpool to Derwenlas, the little port on the Dovey near Machynlleth, thence overland to Gregynog. He allowed himself also the occasional extravagance of a picture—in 1791 he bought one of Powis Castle for £2 2*s.* 6*d.* He also permitted himself

[23] P. Yorke, *The Royal Tribes of Wales*, (ed. R. Williams, Liverpool 1887), pp. 155–8. On uncertain evidence, N.L.W. MS.903C is described as an eighteenth century catalogue of the Gregynog library.

[24] W. Scott Owen, 'Parochial History of Tregynon', art. cit., and for Blayney's making agreements forcing his tenants to agree to rotation of crops, etc., see A. H. Dodd, *Industrial Revolution in North Wales* (Cardiff 1933), p. 37.

[25] The monetary and other accounts in this and the following paragraphs are based on the article of W. Scott Owen, 'Parochial History of Tregynon', *Mont. Colls.*, xxx, 1–168, the latter section of which is based on the various Gregynog account books, some belonging to the early eighteenth century John Blayney, others belonging to Arthur Blayney later on, which still survived as late as 1888 in the Gregynog estate office. N.L.W., Iorwerth C. Peate Deposit Collection. Gregynog Vols. 1–5, Weaver and Blayney accounts 1713 to 1804, vols. 30–34, Blayney estate cash books 1763 to 1795. For the reference to Thomas Percy, Bishop of Dromore, see Sudeley MS. 709.

to be painted by one of the most distinguished portraitists of his day, Sir William Beechey. Only an engraving (copies of which were to be found in many mid-Wales homes in the last century) of this portrait exists at Gregynog today. The original was still in the hands of the Sudeley family at Ham House in 1896, but it has since disappeared. One should not exaggerate the puritanical frugality of his life: his yearly expenses in the year 1773 for instance were £1,402, of which £154 was for his servants (five manservants and five maids) and £372 for running the house, making a total of £1,928. He did keep his horses and beasts in perspective and although he was said to overfeed them, his hounds cost him between £8 and £11 most years. Gregynog did not of course need to be rebuilt in his time, for it was easily large enough for a bachelor and his household. It may be that he altered the house somewhat, for the later eighteenth century sketches of the house which remain, do show Georgian rows of sash-windows in the house. A design of the year 1774 remains[26] which shows a most extensive plan of a Capability Brown type, though by another landscape architect, to replan the whole grounds, with groves and drives and lakes. Some of the project was carried out, and the lakes then designed for Blayney were only later filled in and gardened. Running northwards up the hill, there still exists a great formal avenue or vista cut through the trees, only partially disguised by some informal planting of a later date. This avenue is of the formal gardening school antedating Capability Brown, and it could be that the park around Gregynog had been fairly extensively designed early in the century, and only modernised and made informal in the 1770s by Arthur Blayney. Certainly Blayney had a staff of gardeners at Gregynog, the chief of whom was paid £24 3s. *per annum*, a salary amongst the servants exceeded only by the butler who was paid £31 10s.

Blayney's activities were clear as early as 1772, but in 1777 he came across a most able young man aged twenty, Thomas Colley, whom he decided to appoint as his land agent, or steward.[27] He is said to have been a native of Wellington, but we should remember that a John Colley was a maltster and burgess in Welshpool in 1729, and that the surname is found at Dwyryw, Manafon as far back as 1586-7.[28] Colley was trusted

[26] Gregynog MSS.
[27] W. Scott Owen, art. cit., 140-2, 146-7, for Colley, based partly on local stories and partly on the obituary of Colley in the *Evangelical Magazine* for November 1813.
[28] Sudeley MS. 104.

GREGYNOG, PANELLING OF 1636 IN 'THE BLAYNEY ROOM'

absolutely by Blayney, and he recommended him as part-time agent to other landowners such as squire Proctor of Aberhafesb, and Colley lived with him at Gregynog until 1792 when he moved to Cefngwifed (now Cefn Gwyddfod, hidden on its hilltop from Gregynog by groves of conifers). In 1783 he had become a zealous Methodist, founded a Sunday school at Tregynon church run partly by the rector and partly by himself, he married Jane Bowen of the Methodist family of Tyddyn, Llandinam, and then built at his own expense a chapel for Methodists and dissenters at Tregynon village, which opened in 1798. Although he understood Welsh hardly at all, he gladly attended the Welsh services held there. Besides his importance as a pioneer of dissent and Methodism in those parts, Colley was a most vigorous agent and land improver, and especially after Arthur Blayney's death, pushed forward the movement for enclosing waste lands. Like Blayney his master he was a keen supporter of canals and served on the committee for the Montgomeryshire Canal. Professor Dodd has rightly pointed out Colley's similarity to John Matthews of Mold as improver and Methodist.[29] The new canal, inoculation of children, the growing of turnips, the dissenting chapel, all these were signs of the new age which was to transform Montgomeryshire within a few decades of Blayney's death in 1795, and appear to herald the arrival at Gregynog of a new dynasty.

The new dynasts were in many ways industrialists, and English, and so the dynastic change meant more than the mere replacement of one gentry line by another of the same class. Yorke of Erddig had made much of Blayney's descent over so many centuries from Meilir (whose farm Llwyn Melyn was still an integral part of the Gregynog estate) and of Meilir from the primeval princes of Wales. He would have been comforted had he known that the Hanbury Tracys were descended through Susannah Tracy from the long line of Weavers of Betws, and through them from Gruffydd Deuddwr in the early fifteenth century, and through him from the selfsame Gwennwys and Brochwel Ysgithrog who meant so much to Lewys Dwnn and the bards who had so long drunk the wine of Gregynog that the genealogies had gone to their heads.[30]

[29] A. H. Dodd, *The Industrial Revolution in North Wales*, (Cardiff 1933), p. 67.
[30] I am most grateful to Miss Enid Pierce Roberts for reading the MS. and for saving me from many errors.

CHAPTER FOUR

THE ESTATE AND ITS OWNERS, 1795-1920*

DAVID HOWELL

ARTHUR Blayney, the kindly squire of Gregynog, died unmarried in 1795 at the age of eighty. In his will he devised his estate—not to the Irish Blayneys who had on a certain visit to Gregynog offended him—but to Lord Tracy, who had married Blayney's first cousin, Susannah Weaver (by the time of the will already deceased). Lord Tracy was Henry Tracy, eighth and last Viscount Tracy, owner of the Toddington estate in Gloucestershire. He died two years later, in 1797, leaving an only child and heiress, Henrietta, who on 29 December 1798 married her cousin Charles Hanbury. Charles was the third son of John Hanbury of Pontypool and had assumed by licence on 15 December 1798 the name and arms of Tracy, which was the maiden name both of his future wife and of his grandmother, Jane, daughter of the fifth Viscount Tracy. Charles Hanbury Tracy's marriage gave him possession of Toddington and Gregynog. In 1838 he was raised to the Peerage with the title of Baron Sudeley of Toddington. Gregynog remained in the hands of successive Barons Sudeley until the enforced sale of the estate under the fourth Baron in 1895.[1] The purchaser was Baron James Joicey, who owned Gregynog until 1914 when he, in turn, sold the estate to David Davies of Broneirion and Plas Dinam, and his Company, the Gregynog Estates Limited.[2]

The Sudeleys throughout the nineteenth century looked upon Gregynog as the 'second house' to Toddington. The fourth Baron, for instance, usually spent only August and September there as he found the country about Gregynog too wild for his liking.[3] Gregynog was occupied instead

---

* I would like to thank Mr. Walter Morgan of the National Library of Wales and Dr. Michael Barker, Senior Fellow of the University of Wales, for their help and advice in the preparation of this chapter.

[1] The foregoing is taken from E. Rowley-Morris, 'The Family of Blayney', *Mont. Colls.*, xxi (1887), 273-301, xxii (1888), 71-110; R. Williams, *Montgomeryshire Worthies* (2nd edn., 1894); G. Sandford, 'The House of Gregynog', *Mont. Colls.*, xviii (1885), 229-44.

[2] Abstract of Title of the Gregynog Estates Limited, 1925. This document is housed with the University of Wales solicitors in Cardiff.

[3] Gregynog MSS. Letter of the present Lord Sudeley to the Warden of Gregynog, Dr. Glyn Tegai Hughes, 18 August 1970.

for a long period by the first Lord Sudeley's second son, Henry Hanbury Tracy, who lived there with his wife, Rosamund, from 1840 until his death in 1889.[4] Gregynog, then, played a subordinate role in the family's concerns. Even so the Sudeleys were good landlords to their Welsh tenants, and important participants in Montgomeryshire politics and public affairs generally. Lord Joicey, too, was largely absent from Gregynog, spending most of his time and energies in his vast coal business in the north-east of England. Nevertheless, he continued the Gregynog tradition of supporting the Liberal cause in Montgomeryshire.

The Gregynog estate, in common with all sizeable landed properties in nineteenth-century Britain, was managed by professional agents. As we have seen in an earlier section, Thomas Colley, a Methodist, had energetically served Arthur Blayney for eighteen years, and remained equally industrious under his successors at Gregynog until his death in 1812.[5] He was followed by a Mr. Dyer who managed the property until his death in November 1838 when a Mr. Baker took over,[6] soon to be succeeded, in 1842, by Mr. Scott Owen, who had been trained at Toddington. He remained as agent to Gregynog down to the 1890s. In August 1891 the fourth Lord Sudeley publicly declared to his tenants: 'We are deeply indebted to one gentleman—Mr. Scott Owen—he has done his work admirably; he has done it with tact, discretion and justice, and even during years of agricultural depression he has won your regard and esteem.'[7]

In 1798 the estate covered an area of 7,727 acres. By 1888 it had increased to 18,000 acres,[8] the increase occurring mainly under the first Lord Sudeley who died in 1858. In particular, between 1806 and 1814 lands in Shropshire, including the 10,000 acres at Morville, were sold to enable purchases to be made in Montgomeryshire and Gloucestershire.[9] Most of the Gregynog estate comprised hilly land let out in small sized, family-run farms averaging about fifty acres.

In common with other estates in Britain, the Gregynog rental showed a marked increase during the Napoleonic war period in response to the high prices of these years, and perhaps to some extent reflecting 'how

[4] W. Scott Owen, 'A History of Gregynog Estate, Montgomeryshire', (1888), f. 55.
[5] Id., 'History of Tregynon parish', *Mont. Colls.,* xxx (1896), 1–168.
[6] Gregynog MSS.: Memo Book written by first Lord Sudeley, 1841.
[7] Gregynog MSS.: Newspaper report on the coming of age of Hon. W. C. Hanbury Tracy.
[8] W. Scott Owen, 'A History of Gregynog', ff. 103 and 1.
[9] Gregynog MSS.: Sales and Purchases of first Lord Sudeley.

cheaply his (Mr. Blayney's) farms were let' hitherto.[10] The increase in rents between 1796 and 1815 amounted to 138 per cent.[11] From 1814 prices fell drastically, and there followed down to mid-century, with varying degrees of severity between certain runs of years, a period of stagnation and difficulty for tenant farmers. The heavy rent arrears on the Gregynog estate over these years testify to the depression in the farming industry. Thus between 1838 and 1840 the annual rental of the estate was approximately £11,200. Arrears in 1838 stood at £6,583, in 1839 at £4,165 and in 1840 at £4,267.[12]

From 1853 farming conditions gradually improved throughout Britain. The new demand for agricultural produce from the growing centres of industry pushed up agricultural prices, a peak being reached in the mid 1870s. Better transport facilities provided by railways meant that hitherto remote regions like Wales could now market their surplus produce to these new centres of demand. This more favourable economic climate led many Welsh landlords, like their counterparts elsewhere, to revalue their estates. This was a natural response to new conditions, and does not suggest that landlords were becoming so rapacious and insensitive that they were prepared to exploit the prevalent land hunger of the time. At Gregynog between 1862 and 1885 the rents of certain tenements were raised from between 3 per cent up to 28 per cent, depending upon the previous level of the rent and the location and soil type of the particular farm.[13] Henry Hanbury Tracy reminded Mrs. Owen of Glansevern in 1863 that land values in the favoured parish of Berriew were of necessity higher by as much as three years' purchase than in the wild part of Tregynon parish.[14]

The depression in agriculture in the last quarter of the century did not hit Welsh livestock farmers so seriously as the corn-producing farmers of the Midlands and south-east of England. Nevertheless, Welsh farmers suffered a drop in prices, and in certain years much hardship was endured. Landlords in Wales helped their tenants to ride out the hard times by granting temporary abatements in their rents. The incidence of temporary abatements on the Gregynog estate was as follows: 1884, 5 per cent;

---

[10] Scott Owen, op. cit., f. 106.
[11] National Library of Wales (N.L.W.), Gregynog Estate Rentals in Iorwerth C. Peate Deposit Collection.
[12] Scott Owen, op. cit., f. 103.
[13] Ibid.
[14] N.L.W. Glansevern MS. 7496: letter 17 December 1863.

1885 and 1886, 15 per cent; 1887, 20 per cent; 1888, 7½ per cent; 1890, 5 per cent; 1891, 10 per cent; 1892, 20 per cent; 1893, 20 per cent. As elsewhere in Wales, permanent reductions were on a very limited scale. Thus from 1883 14 per cent on the average were given to fifty-six farms and 10 per cent on five farms.[15] The relative amounts of abatements given from year to year provide a reliable indicator of the intensity of depression at any given time. In common with most other areas of Wales depression here in Montgomeryshire did not create acute anxiety until the early eighties.

Besides the main income from agricultural rents, timber sales from time to time increased the estate income. In 1809, for example, 2,250 oak trees were sold for £15,300. A notable auction of Gregynog timber occurred in 1820 at the Bear's Head, Newtown, when some 2,055 oaks were sold for £19,465.[16] This sale was occasioned by Charles Hanbury Tracy's urgent need of ready cash, since he was about to start building Toddington Manor in Gloucestershire to replace the old decaying Toddington Park.[17] Later, in 1841, when the total rents received were £10,951, sales of timber and bark brought in an extra £8,124.[18]

Before the succession of the fourth Lord Sudeley in 1877 the outlay on repairs and improvements to the Gregynog property was evidently unsatisfactory. A report drawn up for him by a certain Mr. Keary revealed that the various Welsh tenements were badly in need of repairs. 'For many years', wrote the fourth Lord Sudeley, 'the buildings and farm-houses at Gregynog had been patched up and though considerable expense had been annually incurred, it had been done in a very irregular and unsatisfactory manner.'[19] Furthermore, labourers' cottages on the estate were too few. Sudeley therefore embarked upon a heavy programme of expenditure 'in order to prevent the farms from being thrown up'.[20] He availed himself of loans made available by the Lands Improvements Company and under the terms of the Settled Land Act of 1882 in expending some £46,332 between 1878 and 1888 in improvements on farm buildings and drainage on his estate. A further £45,959 was spent in the same

[15] J. E. Vincent, *The Land Question in North Wales* (1896), p. 310, Appendix ii.
[16] Scott Owen, op. cit., f. 109.
[17] M. J. McCarthy, 'Tracy of Toddington Manor', *Transactions of the Bristol and Gloucestershire Archaeological Society*, lxxxiv (1965), 161–74.
[18] Gregynog MSS.: Memo Book of first Lord Sudeley, 1841.
[19] Gregynog MSS.: Historical Summary, 14 July 1893, by 4th Lord Sudeley, contained in a letter of the present Lord Sudeley to Dr. Hughes, 18 August 1970.
[20] Ibid.

period out of his own resources on repairs to farms and other buildings, fencing and gates, making in all some £92,291.[21] With an annual rental of around £12,000, making the total rental from 1878 to 1888 approximately £132,000, the £92,000 or so represented a very high reinvestment of the gross return, some 70 per cent! This, indeed, far exceeded the generous 41 per cent of the gross rental spent by Sir Watkin Williams Wynn on his massive Wynnstay estates in north Wales between 1888 and 1893.[22] The fourth Lord Sudeley claimed that nearly £190,000 had been spent on the Gregynog property over the forty years from 1852-92.

The tenants, then, on the Gregynog estate were generously treated by their landlord in the late years of the century. John Pryse, a leading tenant, could honestly commend Lord Sudeley in a toast he proposed to him at Gregynog in August 1891: 'the whole estate underwent a thorough renovation regardless of cost. Wet cold lands were ordered to be drained upon advantageous terms; cottagers were allowed land to keep a cow where they desired; discount on account of agricultural depression had been allowed.'[23] Not surprisingly, relations between landlord and tenant were harmonious at Gregynog throughout the last century. Although the majority of holdings were held yearly, there were many families in the 1890s who had been resident on the estate for generations.[24]

Farm labourers' cottage accommodation was extremely inadequate in late-nineteenth-century Wales. A report in the early 1890s on the overall cottage situation in Britain observed: 'It would seem that bad as the cottage accommodation is in some parts of England, it is far worse in Wales. The general standard of accommodation is lower, and there is much less evidence of progress and improvement.'[25] Cottages built on the Gregynog estate furnished a noticeable exception to this general state of affairs. In all some forty new cottages were built there between 1842 and 1892, twenty-five of which were constructed after 1874. Furthermore, all the old cottages on the estate had been repaired by 1892.[26] Thomas Nicholas remarked in 1872 that the resident of Gregynog, Henry Hanbury Tracy, acting on behalf of the third Lord Sudeley, had 'set to the landowners of Wales an example in cottage building' which, if followed,

[21] Scott Owen, op. cit., ff. 130-40.
[22] Vincent, op. cit., pp. 226-7.
[23] Gregynog MSS.: newspaper report of coming of age of Hon. W. C. Hanbury Tracy.
[24] Gregynog MSS.: Letter 4 November 1892 of 4th Lord Sudeley to Geo. M. Owen.
[25] Parliamentary Papers, 1894, xxxv, Section B, p. 220.
[26] Royal Commission on Land in Wales and Monmouthshire, vol. 5, Appendix 10.

would vastly improve 'the health, morals and comfort of the people.'
The whole structure, including the roof, was built with concrete rather
than stone or brick, and at just over half the normal cost involved. Once
constructed, there was little risk of deterioration.

Given the state of the fourth Lord Sudeley's finances, this tremendous
outlay at Gregynog was ill-advised, and helped towards his financial
collapse in the early 1890s and the consequent sale of Gregynog. The
position of Gregynog is understandable only when seen in the wider
context of the fourth Lord Sudeley's commitments at Toddington and
elsewhere.[27] The third Lord Sudeley died in 1877 leaving a debt of nearly
£100,000, which his successor, rather than repudiate, decided to shoulder
by borrowing the money from Insurance Offices, facing thereby annual
interest and premium repayments of between £7,000 and £8,000 a year.
On top of this, family charges, drawn up in the marriage settlements,
amounted to £5,000 a year. In spite of this crippling financial burden,
Sudeley over the twelve years following 1877 recklessly laid out about
£160,000 on improvements and drainage at Toddington and Gregynog.
Writing in 1893 he acknowledged his mistake in not accurately ascertaining
what income might be fairly expected from the intended outlay. He
admitted to thinking that the small income on his accession was due
mainly to poor management as the Estates had apparently paid well in
past years. What he failed to realise, he lamented, was that the general
income had been made up previously from other sources and by
encroaching on capital. Thus the second and third Lords Sudeley, his
father and brother respectively, had whittled away a large personal
property of railway securities on unremunerative improvements. Any
further improvements would, of necessity, have to be financed from
borrowed capital, and Sudeley admitted his folly in pursuing this course.
In retrospect he claimed that he should not have shouldered his brother's
debts, that all expenses should have been avoided and that both estates
should have been let.

Instead he resorted to temporary expedients at different times. Thus the
London house was let for six years. Gregynog mansion and shootings
were let for five years and, on one occasion, Toddington mansion and
shootings were lent to a relation who paid all expenses. But such

[27] The information that follows on Sudeley's difficulties is taken from Gregynog MSS.: Historical
Summary, 14 July 1893, op. cit.

economies were of little help in the face of his heavy outgoings. The net rental of both estates jointly yielded £7,000 and his private income added another £3,000, making a total of £10,000 a year. Against this, family charges were £5,000 a year, brother's debts, interest and premiums £7,000, and expenses of the establishment whilst living at Toddington, Gregynog and in London some £7,000 to £8,000 a year. Thus a heavy deficit was annually incurred.

Sudeley also endeavoured to increase his income by means of industrial pursuits, and in 1881 he joined Sir William Armstrong's gunnery Company whose London manager until 1880 had been (significantly as we shall see) Stuart Rendel. Before inheriting Gregynog, the fourth Lord Sudeley had become chairman of the Welsh Woollen Manufacturing Co., and upon his inheritance in 1877 he increased his stake in it. Concurrently he began fruit culture at Toddington. Both ventures proved expensive failures. In the case of the former, orders were difficult to obtain because of the distance of the woollen factory at Newtown from the seat of the flannel and tweed trade. Also bad management led to too much money being paid for the wrong kind of wool. By 1882 the Company was forced to go into liquidation and Sudeley, foolishly shouldering alone the large debt, lost no less than £100,000. He resuscitated the business as the Severn Tweed Co., but owing to the depression of trade the venture collapsed and finally went into liquidation in 1892. The same sad story of mismanagement applied to his extensive orchards in the Vale of Evesham. In all £40,000 was squandered on the Toddington Orchard Co., but worse was to follow. Before the fruit trees had time to come into full bearing he became bankrupt, and this insolvency entailed another severe loss.

Sudeley's losses in these two ventures unhappily coincided with agricultural depression, which reached its peak in the early 1890s. As we have seen, farm rents at Gregynog had to be temporarily abated and a few permanently reduced, and so no return of interest in the form of increased rents on the heavy capital outlays on improvements was possible.

Sudeley made a last bid to rescue his fortune by going into the City where he became a Director of the Projectile Co., and of Murietta & Co. But the depression in trade, and his being outmanoeuvred by financial sharks, once again led to heavy losses. As a last resort in 1892 he asked his wife to borrow money, but this was done to no avail, except to cripple her income and finally alienate him in her affections. His business ineptitude, sheer bad luck, and foolish generosity in shouldering other people's losses meant that the Gregynog property, heavily encumbered along with Toddington since the Resettlement of 1891, was put up for sale in 1894. The gossip in Montgomeryshire in the summer of 1895 was that Lady Sudeley, looking "old and haggard", had offered to buy Gregynog from the Receivers.[28] This was not to be so, and the eventual purchaser in 1895 was James, Baron Joicey, a great north country coal owner, who may well have been influenced in his purchase by Stuart Rendel. Both had businesses on Tyneside and both were prominent Liberals (in fact they were Parliamentary colleagues). Unfortunately, there appears to be no information about the economic affairs of the Gregynog property under Joicey.

We must now consider the house at Gregynog and the political and social activities of the families who owned it over these years. It is not clear who occupied Gregynog Hall before 1840. In that year, as already noted, Henry Hanbury Tracy and his wife went to live there. After residing there for a few years, he became so dissatisfied with its comforts (it was very old and overrun with rats) that he intended leaving. But Sudeley was anxious for his son to remain, and accordingly carried out alterations so extensive that a completely new house was built. Although the new house was erected on the same foundations as the old one, the rooms were now larger and an upper storey was added to what had formerly been a ground and bedroom floor residence. The house was changed out of all recognition, but its fine old carved parlour, dating back to the time of Charles I, was retained.[29] The approach leading to the hall was subsequently altered a number of times. In 1880, the water-logged approach along the centre of the Wern Bottom was replaced by the imposing drive which exists at present. The ground was stoned, widened and fenced in, and a new concrete bridge built over the depression in front of the house. On the east side of the bridge the drive was continued to the Tregynon cross roads.[30]

[28] N.L.W. Rendel MS. 14 (N.L.W. MS. 19465C), No. 670: Letter 29 September 1895 of Humphreys Owen to Rendel.
[29] Scott Owen, op. cit., ff. 56–7; Lord Sudeley, 'Gregynog before the year 1900', *Mont. Colls.,* lxii (1971), p. 179
[30] Gregynog MSS.: Letter 24 April 1969 of Lady Marshall-Cornwall to Dr. Hughes.

The Hanbury Tracy family, though non-resident for much of the time, played an important rôle in Montgomeryshire affairs in the last century, particularly in the second half. Charles Hanbury Tracy (created first Lord Sudeley in 1838) was one of the foremost promoters of the Montgomery-shire canal, in which he held fifty shares.[31] The canal reached Newtown in 1819, and henceforth this waterway afforded easy carriage for timber sold off the well-wooded Gregynog estate. He was also closely involved in the improvement of turnpike roads within the County. As M.P. for Tewkesbury he voted for the Reform Bill of 1832, and at the following election he participated fully in the Montgomeryshire Boroughs contest. The constituency was seething with excitement, and Charles was instru-mental in securing the return of Sir John Edwards, a progressive liberal, over the Tory candidate.[32]

It has been shown that the woollen mills in Newtown owed a great deal to the family. By the 1860s the industry was in desperate straits, and could only be rescued from certain extinction by drastic modernisation. In 1865 Charles Douglas Richard Hanbury Tracy played a leading rôle in the formation of the Cambrian Flannel Co., which acquired the Cambrian mill, the largest in Newtown, employing 500-600 workpeople.[33] No doubt he poured money into the industry in order to buy electoral support,[34] but his continuing interest even after moving to the Upper House in 1877 reveals that he also looked upon the venture in a public-spirited way. At a yearly rent audit in 1893 the estate agent of his political and trading rival, Sir Pryce Jones, expressed sympathy for his financial losses, declaring that he had supported the trade for the public weal rather than private gain.[35]

In politics the family stands out as a pillar of the Liberal cause in Montgomeryshire. The Hanbury family came of Whig stock, and in 1832 Charles Hanbury Tracy naturally supported Reform. On the death of Mr. David Pugh in 1861, Captain Charles George Hanbury Tracy, eldest son of the second Baron Sudeley by his wife Emma Pennant of Penrhyn Castle, came forward as the Liberal candidate for the Montgomeryshire Boroughs, but he did not force a contest at the polls. A Conservative was

[31] Glansevern MS. 10776: Montgomeryshire Canal Proprietors' Shares; Sandford, art. cit., p. 241.
[32] O. Ashton, 'Chartism in mid Wales', *Mont. Colls.,* lxii (1971), 16; Sandford, art. cit., 241.
[33] Lord Sudeley 'Gregynog before the year 1900', art. cit., 181.
[34] Gregynog MSS.: Letter of E. R. Morris, 7 November 1967 to Lord Sudeley.
[35] Lord Sudeley, 'Gregynog before the year 1900', art. cit., 181-2.

returned unopposed. However, he did fight the Montgomeryshire seat in June 1862 against the formidable Conservative candidate, Mr. Charles Watkin Williams Wynn, who defeated him by 307 votes. Seemingly the Wynn family had not expected this victory, for Miss Charlotte Williams Wynn wrote to Baroness Bunsen: 'Then came the terrible accident that killed my cousin Colonel Williams Wynn, and in consequence my brother's election. It was a hotly contested one, and I had no hope that he would gain it, so that a majority of nearly 300 was the more astonishing.'[36] No doubt the family was fully aware of the widespread ill-feeling aroused against itself over the 1859 ejection of tenants on their Merioneth Rhiwlas estate. But Captain Charles could not capitalise upon this growing feeling of resentment. In February 1863 his parliamentary aspirations came to an abrupt end with the death of his father, and he became the third Lord Sudeley.

His brother was Charles Douglas Richard Hanbury Tracy, who in August 1863, after a severe contest with Major C. V. Pugh over the vacant seat, was elected M.P. for the Montgomeryshire Boroughs.[37] He was supported during the campaign by his uncle, Henry Hanbury Tracy of Gregynog, who canvassed, for example, the support of the influential Humphreys Owen family of Glansevern.[38] He retained the seat until his succession to the peerage as fourth Lord Sudeley in 1877. A newspaper report of the 1860s shows him as an extraordinary character. After he had been M.P. for three years his constituents urged upon him the necessity for raising money to build an infirmary at Newtown. Upon considering many devices how the necessary funds could be collected, Tracy decided to raise part of the sum himself. He took lessons from a professional conjurer and, disguised by means of false hair, he visited Newtown in March 1867 as the 'Wizard of the West'. He entertained his constituents for two hours and no one was aware of his identity until he mentioned the fact a few days later. In this way £50 was raised, and gradually sufficient sums were obtained by public subscription for the infirmary to be built.[39]

[36] Williams, op. cit., pp. 301–2.
[37] W. R. Williams, *Parliamentary History of Wales* (1895), p. 152; *The Times*, 11 December 1922: Obituary of Fourth Baron Sudeley.
[38] Glansevern MS. 7082: Letter of H. H. Tracy to Mrs. A. W. Owen, 28 July 1863.
[39] Gregynog MSS.: Newspaper report.

Early in his parliamentary career this same Charles D. R. Hanbury Tracy ran into trouble with his constituents over his attitude towards the second Reform Bill. In the spring of 1866 he voted in favour of Lord Grosvenor's amendment, which attempted to couple redistribution of seats with the change in the franchise. Montgomeryshire people wrongly interpreted this as signifying his opposition to all reform.[40] Shortly afterwards he offended his constituents still further by supporting Lord Dunkellin's amendment, which placed the franchise on a rating instead of a rental basis. Hanbury Tracy considered the change 'a mere matter of detail' involving 'no vital point connected with the Bill, as we were fully prepared to support such a reduction as would admit the number of voters contemplated by the government'. But the government's defeat by eleven votes on this amendment led them to resign. Hanbury Tracy reflected: 'I must confess that if it had been stated clearly that the Government would not have consented to the alteration, my vote would not have been given against them.' He understandably refused to attend meetings at Newtown and Welshpool to explain his whole conduct, preferring to wait a few months until tempers had cooled.[41] Despite these early difficulties, he continued active in Borough politics as member down to 1877. In 1876 he was exerting pressure upon A. C. Humphreys Owen of Glansevern to contest the County seat at the next election, offering him £2,000 towards this and the promise of a further £2,000 later.[42]

His removal to the Lords as fourth Lord Sudeley in 1877 left the door open for his younger brother, Frederick Stephen Archibald Hanbury Tracy, to contest the vacant Boroughs seat in May 1877 against Viscount Castlereagh. He was successful by 329 votes.[43] His residence in Montgomeryshire from the summer of 1878 was a 'little house', Penbryn.[44] In the late 1870s both the fourth Lord Sudeley and F. S. A. Hanbury Tracy, along with Humphreys Owen of Glansevern, were campaigning for Stuart Rendel's entry into Montgomeryshire politics and, as is well known, in April 1880 Rendel was elected Liberal M.P. for the County. In early September 1878 Rendel was a guest at Gregynog[45] and, later,

[40] Glansevern MS. 7077: Letter of Charles Hanbury Tracy to Mrs. A. W. Owen, 2 May 1866.
[41] Ibid., MS. 7258: Letter of Charles Hanbury Tracy to Mrs. A. W. Owen, 5 July 1866.
[42] Ibid., MS. 5419: Letter of A. C. Humphreys Owen to his father, 14 November 1876.
[43] Williams, op. cit., p. 152.
[44] Rendel Letters and Papers, letter 155: F. S. A. Hanbury Tracy to Rendel, 17 September 1878.
[45] Ibid., letter 154: F. S. A. Hanbury Tracy to Rendel, 11 September 1878.

on 22 September Sudeley wrote to Rendel: 'Lady Sudeley is writing to try and persuade you and Mrs. Rendel to come here on Monday the 30 to Wednesday the 2 October. We are going into Newtown on the evening of the 30th for Mr. Prandron's reading and on Tuesday we have invited half the County to hear him at Gregynog. A splendid opportunity for the County Member!'[46] F. S. A. Hanbury Tracy wrote letters to Rendel in the autumn of 1878 informing him of favourable feelings in the County towards his candidature.[47] As we shall see, relations of both men with Rendel were later to become estranged.

F. S. A. Hanbury Tracy was re-elected to the Boroughs seat in April 1880, triumphing over the Tory woollen-manufacturer, Pryce Jones of Dolerw, Newtown.[48] A meeting was held at Newtown on 10 April to celebrate the twin victories of Tracy and Rendel. David Davies of Llandinam, elected unopposed for the Cardigan Boroughs on 6 April, attended and made a speech: 'you know there are some old fogies in the county always trying to marry their daughters to some old man the ladies don't love. Well these boroughs tried to thrust Mr. Pryce Jones on us, but we didn't love him and therefore we didn't marry him. We have now Mr. Tracy, a man after our own hearts, and we have married him again for seven years. We are proud of him not only because he is a handsome man, but he is one of the right sort and gives his vote right in the House of Commons, the same as Old Davies, Llandinam, does.'[49]

The tables were turned in November 1885 when Pryce Jones was elected for the Boroughs.[50] When Gladstone introduced his Irish Home Rule bill into Parliament in the following spring, the Liberal ranks were everywhere thrown into disarray. Montgomeryshire was no exception. The national crisis was sure to provide a sudden general election, and Lord Sudeley disliked Gladstone's policy so much that he informed the Boroughs Liberal Association that he intended to withdraw from local politics, cut off the supply of funds to the local party, and ignore the existence of his son's candidature.[51] Accordingly, on 20 April 1886 Rendel was urging upon A. C. Humphreys Owen that F. S. A. Hanbury Tracy ought to declare whether or not he would stand at his own expense

[46] Ibid., letter 156: Fourth Lord Sudeley to Rendel, 22 September 1878.
[47] Ibid., letters 157 and 158.
[48] Williams, op. cit., p. 153.
[49] I. Thomas, Top Sawyer (1938), pp. 224-6.
[50] Williams, op. cit., p. 153.
[51] Glansevern MS. 237: Letter of Rendel to Humphreys Owen, 14 April 1886.

as a Gladstonian Liberal. Certainly he, Rendel, having 'spent £14,000 hard cash in political outgoings over the last seven years', was not prepared to help finance Tracy's election campaign.[52] The situation was still unresolved in early June. Humphreys Owen wrote to Rendel on 11 June: 'Will he (Sudeley) relent at last to Tracy?'[53] In mid-June it appeared that Sudeley and Tracy were in agreement over backing a compromise candidate, a certain Mr. Roche, whose claim, they judged, would not later stand in Tracy's way. Rendel was vexed at this, insisting that if Tracy and Sudeley felt disposed to participate it should have been as principals. He accused Tracy of mismanaging the whole affair, and argued that much embarrassment and difficulty would have been avoided had Tracy been straightforward and retired at the time of deciding not to stand.[54] By early July the situation had resolved itself, Fairless Humphreys making way for Tracy, who successfully contested the seat against Pryce Jones.[55]

Further trouble and embitterment were to follow, which reached a climax in 1893. By April 1887 Tracy was informing A. C. Humphreys Owen that he could not afford to remain in Parliament and was about to resign.[56] The Liberal leaders were talking of either Fairless Humphreys or G. O. Trevelyan (a defeated ex-cabinet minister) contesting the vacant seat.[57] By 21 April Tracy had resigned, claiming that he needed all his money for his children's education and his business interests like his Gas Light Company (reputed to be a swindle)[58] and flannel company. He informed Humphreys Owen that he intended staying on for the present Parliament, but stated that in the meantime he would not stand in anyone's way. Humphreys Owen had by now become exasperated with his shifting conduct, and wrote to Rendel: 'I think he is all on the surfaces and is a nice spoiled child', and 'he does not set much store by the seat and is eager for anything that may be to his advantage'.[59] By January 1888, however, Tracy had again accepted nomination to stand in the next election, a concession he claimed, extracted from him much against his

[52] Ibid., MS. 240: Letter 20 April 1886.
[53] Rendel MS. 14 (N.L.W. MS. 19461C): Letter 289.
[54] Glansevern MS. 255: Letter of Rendel to Humphreys Owen, 20 June 1886.
[55] Williams, op. cit., p. 153.
[56] Rendel MS. 14 (N.L.W. MS. 19462C): Letter 340: A. C. Humphreys Owen to Rendel, 7 April 1887.
[57] Ibid., letter 344: A. C. Humphreys Owen to Rendel, 14 April 1887; see also K. O. Morgan, *Wales in British Politics* (2nd edn. 1971), p. 81. Dr. Morgan aptly labels Tracy 'the frivolous whig'.
[58] Rendel MS. 14, letter 347: A. C. Humphreys Owen to Rendel, 20 April 1887.
[59] Ibid., letter 349: 21 April 1887.

own wish by the solicitations of his constituents.[60] Humphreys Owen wrote to Rendel in April 1889: 'I have never been able to understand Tracy and therefore cannot sympathise with him. Whether he really meant to play fast and loose I don't know, but what we saw of his conduct could not be explained in any other way.'[61] Rendel by this time was under no illusions: 'Tracy', he confided to Humphreys Owen, 'expects to draw upon me when he chooses and drop me when he chooses and to be nasty in any case in which I didn't meet his views.'[62]

The election in the Boroughs on 8 July 1892 was fought between F. S. A. Hanbury Tracy and Pryce Jones. Tracy was defeated, and although a petition was presented against Jones's return it was dismissed after a trial lasting a few days. In January 1893 the Montgomeryshire Central Liberal Association invited Tracy to contest the Boroughs seat at the next election.[63] He replied that he could not accept the invitation, but at the same time held himself free to come forward when he so wished independent of party feeling. 'If you can find anyone', he wrote, 'willing to come forward knowing that I may present myself at any moment you had better immediately select him.'[64] In many letters to the Association he gave reasons for his unwillingness to pledge his support at that time one way or the other. He blamed his defeat of the previous year on the failure of the party to support him fully, certain people subordinating their political principles to their personal animosities.[65] In particular, he reserved his bitterest anger for Humphreys Owen who, he claimed, had told him before the previous election that he could not support him fully because of family connections.[66] Such accusations were emphatically refuted by the Association, but there is no question that he felt able to act independently because of this alleged lack of previous support. Secondly, Tracy was dissatisfied with the attitude of the Gladstonian Liberal Government with regard to questions affecting Wales and now held back from committing himself to their future policy. For instance, he complained, the question of the Disestablishment of the Church in Wales, though a prominent feature in the Newcastle programme, found

[60] Ibid., Rendel MS. 14 (N.L.W. MS. 19463C): Letter 410: A. C. Humphreys Owen to Rendel, 3 January 1888.
[61] Ibid., letter 482: 24 April 1889.
[62] Glansevern MS. 529: Letter 22 April 1891.
[63] Rendel MS. 167 and Glansevern MS. 8109.
[64] Rendel MS. 167: Letter of F. S. A. Hanbury Tracy to Mr. Jones, 11 January 1893.
[65] Glansevern MS. 8110: Letter of F. S. A. Hanbury Tracy to Mr. Lloyd, 16 January 1893.
[66] Ibid., MS. 6199: Letter of F. S. A. Hanbury Tracy to Humphreys Owen, 17 June 1893.

no place in the policy of the Government as indicated in the Queen's speech.[67] He fatuously claimed that the fact that he was opposed to the Suspensory Bill as an unfair attack on 'my Church' did not in any way lessen his support for Disestablishment and Disendowment.[68]

Tracy's conduct was open to differing interpretations. A number of supporters accepted these explanations and remained loyal to the last. The leadership of the Montgomeryshire Liberal Association was, not surprisingly, critical. Rendel believed that Tracy realised the Liberal Party in London would no longer finance him as previously, and so he was now looking to Unionism as his only hope: 'His main point, personally, is the Exchequer. His reservation of his right to stand in either the Liberal or Unionist side is, I think, designed to enable him (if accepted) to draw money from one party by threatening to stand in the interest of the other.'[69] His 'shabbiness and self-intrigue' deeply angered Rendel.[70] The quarrel between Tracy and the Montgomeryshire Liberal Association was openly waged in the press. Support for Tracy from people like Richard Lloyd, chairman of the Newtown Liberal 'Three Hundred',[71] meant that the situation in the Boroughs remained unsettled, no Liberal candidate having been agreed upon by January 1894.[72] Ultimately the Liberal group of Humphreys Owen and Rendel found the only way to get rid of Tracy was to 'give' the seat to the enemy.[73] In 1895 Major E. Pryce Jones, Conservative, beat O. C. Philipps, Gladstonian Liberal, by 1,435 votes to 1,351. Tracy did not again stand for election but he continued to play a part in Borough politics. A. C. Humphreys Owen informed Rendel in November 1899 that Baron James Joicey, owner of Gregynog since 1895, had told him that he had suggested Tracy as a candidate for the Boroughs. 'We (Mrs. O. and I) gave him an outline of the fellow's proceedings in 1892 and he said he would not as he intended write to Herbert Gladstone to suggest him. Joicey said he had met F. Tracy lately and asked him if he was going to stand and his answer was that he was doubtful. We have had a narrow escape for Joicey knew nothing about Tracy's career.'[74]

[67] Ibid., MS. 8116: Letter of F. S. A. Hanbury Tracy to Mr. Jones, 11 February 1893.
[68] Ibid., MS. 8117: Letter of F. S. A. Hanbury Tracy to Mr. Jones, 11 February 1893.
[69] Ibid., MS. 628: Letter of Rendel to Humphreys Owen, 22 May 1893.
[70] Ibid., MS. 8122: Letter of Rendel to Mr. Jones, 23 January 1893.
[71] *Montgomeryshire County Times*, 8 and 29 July 1893.
[72] Glansevern MS. 646: Letter of Rendel to Humphreys Owen, 27 January 1894.
[73] Ibid., MS. 785: Letter of Rendel to Humphreys Owen, 8 June 1903.
[74] Rendel MS. 14 (N.L.W. MS. 19466C): Letter 686e, 28 November 1899.

Lord Sudeley continued to play an important part in County politics after his elevation to the peerage in 1877. He was one of the inner circle responsible for the selection of the Liberal candidate for the County seat. In 1886, however, he fell out with Gladstone over Irish Home Rule. Nevertheless he agreed to lend Gregynog Hall in October 1888 to Rendel to entertain Morley on the occasion of an important political meeting in Wales in support of Home Rule. Sudeley was quick to point out in *The Times*, however, that this did not mean that he supported the Gladstonian wing of the Party over its Irish policy. He ostentatiously declined an invitation to take part in the proceedings of the meeting, holding that the restoration of law and order in Ireland was necessary before any further remedial measures could be considered. Morley informed Rendel on 5 October 1888 that following this paragraph in *The Times* he could not stay at Gregynog.[75] Apart from Cornwallis-West, Sudeley was the only Welsh Liberal of note who subscribed to the view of Joseph Chamberlain (the leading English Liberal Unionist) that Gladstone's obsession with Home Rule was in reality a cynical attempt to postpone Welsh Disestablishment indefinitely.[76]

Further alienation from the Gladstonian wing arose over Gladstone's views on the Welsh Land problem. In *The Times* of 19 September 1892, Sudeley attacked Gladstone's assertion that English landowners had reduced their rents far more generously than had their Welsh counterparts during the farming depression years from the late 1870s. He justifiably pointed to the difference in circumstances between the large arable farms of eastern England, severely hit by low corn prices, and the small family-run pastoral farms of Wales, which were not so badly affected. He concluded his letter: ' . . . being connected with land in both England and Wales, I am able to deny most emphatically that Welsh landlords are open to censure; but on the contrary, I am positive that they have met their tenants in as kindly a manner and with as considerable reductions as landlords in England, though such alterations in rent may have been on a different basis.' Later, on 4 November, Sudeley, writing to George Owen, Secretary of the North Wales Landowners' Defence Association, referred to 'the Land Cry which they (the Gladstonian wing) are now making such good use of for party purposes'.[77] Sudeley's belief that a

[75] Rendel MSS. 575 and 576: Letters of Morley, 5 October 1888.
[76] Morgan, op. cit., p. 79.
[77] Gregynog MSS.

Welsh land problem existed only in the minds of demagogic Radical politicians, brought him into direct conflict with Gladstone and the majority of Welsh Liberal leaders led by Tom Ellis.

In the 1890s relations between Sudeley and Rendel inevitably deteriorated, both politically and socially. However, in 1902, Lady Sudeley, despite her estranged relations with her husband (albeit, living under the same roof) arranged for a reconciliation of sorts.[78] Sudeley's letter to Rendel on 30 November 1902, written from his new abode at Ormeley Lodge, Surrey, struck a penitent note: 'I have greatly regretted our estrangement and there is no one I should like to be on friendly terms again more than yourself. Alas I know it is my own fault but we live and learn.'[79]

Sudeley's successor at Gregynog, Lord Joicey, was once again an absentee, spending most of his time in his coal business in the north-east of England. He was a faithful follower of Gladstone, and sat for Chester-le-Street from 1885 to 1905, in which year he was made a peer. However, Joicey's Radical convictions began to waver as soon as he entered the upper house (and in this respect he merely followed the example of many elderly politicians who owed their elevation solely to the generosity of successive Liberal governments). From 1906 he watched developments in Liberal policy with grave misgivings. In 1909 his unwillingness to support the Budget led him to resign the presidency of the Montgomeryshire Boroughs Liberal Association.[80]

Gregynog, Powis Castle and Plas Machynlleth were the three stately homes dominating County Society in the nineteenth century. Shooting parties, the hunt, social visits to and from neighbouring families, were all important events in the lives of the landed classes. As was commonly the case elsewhere, detailed lists of game killed for each year after 1851[81] were recorded for the Gregynog properties, and game rights were jealously guarded. A bitter dispute arose between the Sudeleys and Sir Watkin Williams Wynn of Wynnstay over the shooting rights on a portion of the Gregynog estate, a quarrel which was only finally settled in 1885.[82] The coming of age of the eldest son was always the occasion

[78] Rendel MS. 163: Letter to Rendel of 25 November 1902.
[79] Ibid., MS. 164.
[80] *The Times,* 23 November 1936: Obituary Notice.
[81] Scott Owen, op. cit., f. 128.
[82] Ibid., ff. 121–8.

of maximum rejoicing on landed estates, and such an event occurred at Gregynog in August 1891 with the twenty-first birthday of the Hon. Wilfrid Charles Hanbury Tracy, eldest son of the fourth Lord Sudeley. The day's proceedings commenced with a procession of local inhabitants which, with the Gregynog Brass Band and a fat ox at its head, marched from the Temperance House, Tregynon, to the Hall. After cheering in front of the Hall, the procession returned to the fields where the ox was cut up and distributed. The tenants of the estate meanwhile, at 12.30, sat down to a banquet in a pavilion with Lord Sudeley and his friends. From 3 to 7 o'clock Lady Sudeley held an 'at-home', and from 5 to 6 o'clock there was a fashionable garden party. The villagers meanwhile spent their time upon the fields. Some 2,500 sat down to tea after which sports were held. The evening was rounded off with a fireworks display.[83]

On 25 March 1914 Lord Joicey sold a 'large portion', some 7,403 acres, of the Gregynog estate to David Davies, M.P. of Broneirion and Plas Dinam, in the parish of Llandinam, and the Gregynog Estates Limited Company whose offices were at Llandinam. On 29 July 1915 the Company, in order to raise a loan of £45,000 with the intention of consolidating this borrowed sum into one Stock carrying interest at $4\frac{1}{2}$ per cent, mortgaged the Gregynog property to Edward Jones of Maesmawr Hall, Caersws, in Montgomeryshire, and two others as trustees. From this date up to 24 July 1920 portions of the mortgaged premises were sold by the Company with the concurrence of the Trustees and the purchase money was paid to the Trustees in part discharge of the Debenture Stock. By 24 July 1920 the Company had paid the whole of the money borrowed on 29 July 1915, and the Trustees thereby reconveyed to the Company the Gregynog property with the exception of what had been sold between 1915 and 1920.[84] In early March 1920 a six days' sale occurred of the contents of the Gregynog Hall by the direction of the Gregynog Estates Limited.[85] Buyers attended from all over Britain to purchase the 2,500 or so lots. In April some 2,000 acres of the outlying portions of the Estate were put up for sale, first preference being given to sitting tenants who wished to purchase their holdings.[86] Some 1,400 acres were actually sold to sitting tenants, and the remaining 600 acres were sold on 31

[83] Gregynog MSS.: Newspaper reports.
[84] Abstract of Title of the Gregynog Estates Limited to freehold lands in Montgomeryshire.
[85] *Montgomeryshire Express*, 9 March 1920.
[86] *Montgomeryshire County Times*, 17 April 1920.

August 1920.[87] On 31 July 1920 the Gregynog Estates Limited sold Gregynog Hall, with 311 adjoining acres in Tregynon parish, to Gwendoline Elizabeth Davies and Margaret Davies, spinster sisters, both of Plas Dinam, for £33,599.[88] It appears that Gwendoline Davies talked during the first World War (in France in 1917), with Dora Herbert Jones, of founding a sort of craft centre in Wales, even mentioning Gregynog as a possibility.[89] The brother of the Davies sisters was David Davies of Plas Dinam (created Lord Davies in 1932) whose Company, as we have seen, owned Gregynog from 1914. They were thus in a favourable position to purchase the mansion and grounds in 1920.

[87] Ibid., 31 July 1920 and 4 September 1920.
[88] Document housed at University of Wales solicitors, Cardiff.
[89] Information given to Dr. Prys Morgan in conversation with Dora Herbert Jones.

CHAPTER FIVE

LIFE AT GREGYNOG BETWEEN THE WARS

PRYS MORGAN

WILLIAM Morris the author and craftsman died in 1896, when Gwendoline Davies was in her teens, and when Margaret was a mere child. Like the Davies sisters Morris was both a product of the Victorian capitalist society and a reaction to it.

In Morris's life there had been a brave attempt to combine arts and crafts with a devotion to high minded good causes; he founded the Kelmscott Press to produce beautiful books; and anyone who visits Kelmscott Manor today, where much of Morris's furniture from his London house is preserved, has the uncanny feeling of similarity to Gregynog, the same taste for unpretentious oak furniture, simple old coffers, enlivened by the highly personal or unconventional exotic; at Kelmscott we find simple old Dutch and Chinese pots, at Gregynog a superb Kuwaiti chest and some early Islamic vases. The parallel must not be driven too far, for instead of Morris's joyous socialism we have the Presbyterian puritanism of the Davieses, and instead of Morris's medievalism, we find the Davieses' delight in the French art of their own time. There were naturally sources other than the Morris circle for the tastes of the Davieses. The Bloomsbury circle, whom the Davieses knew very faintly through Thomas Jones's acquaintance with David Garnett, also shared their delight in modern French art, still a rather *recherché* taste in the twenties, although French art had been an enthusiasm of the English Aesthetic movement (which was connected with the Morris circle if not Morris directly) back in the 1870s and 80s. There were other country houses with music festivals, such as Mr. Christie's Glyndebourne, other country houses with art and craft communities such as Dartington Hall in Devon, but there was no house quite like Gregynog nor aesthetes quite like the Davies sisters anywhere.

It may be that Thomas Jones, their friend and mentor, a sage whom the sisters found instructive and incorruptible, had conveyed to them some of the Morris ideals. It may be that this combination of high idealism with love of the arts was the only kind of bohemianism or aestheticism possible for this first generation to grow up after the great Welsh Victorian crusades. The generation of pulpit giants had given rise to the generation of the National Library, National Museum, and the University, and that a half generation before the Davieses were born; Sir Owen M. Edwards with his passionate desire to make the Welshman see things anew, and to fill the Welshman's books with pictures; Sir John Morris Jones had a Morrisian enthusiasm for honest craftsmanship, both in words and in real handiwork; Sir Herbert Lewis (to whom Dora Herbert Jones was private secretary long before she came to Gregynog) had a passion for beautiful books, as did Principal J. H. Davies, and the instances could be multiplied, so much so that we can observe a whole circle of Welsh society longing to give the land of the saints a seeing eye. If the Davieses reacted against Welsh Victorian philistinism, they were certainly not alone in this.

It is hard to know exactly why the sisters together with their brother David Davies (later first Lord Davies) came to purchase Gregynog in 1914. Gwendoline had apparently known the house since her youth for until she came under the influence of a very high-minded cousin who changed her tastes, she had been a keen huntswoman and had come to Gregynog to hunt. Her brother never lost his passion for hunting, he had started a fine pack of hounds and the hunt which bears his name still meets regularly a few miles away from Gregynog, and it may be that he was interested in the value of the estate for hunting and shooting. The two sisters may simply have wished to save the house from demolition. There was a rumour that some parts of Gregynog, probably the Carved Parlour, would be torn out and shipped to some 'Citizen Kane' across the Atlantic. Maybe Thomas Jones whom they had known at Newtown since 1910 had planted the seed of a Morrisian craft guild in their minds; their formidable and lively stepmother Mrs. Edward Davies shared a number of the sisters' ideals.

Dora Herbert Jones recalled that in about 1916 or 1917 when she worked with Gwendoline Davies in her unit to help the troops in Northern France, Gwendoline intended that Gregynog might one day become the home of a craft guild or community. At this time the house was apparently rented to rich tenants who caused no small distress to the Davieses by devoting the dingle or dell gardens to breeding dogs. Meanwhile the war in Northern France took their minds off such matters.

After the Great War the Davieses were all deeply involved in various schemes and plans to lay the foundations, as they thought, of a new Wales. Gregynog was to become a craft and conference centre for Wales, and should be seen as merely one part of the family's great project. By 1920 the house became vacant and was put up for sale, and though it must have been prearranged that the two sisters should buy it from the limited company which had hitherto owned it, the furnishings which remained were sold; for there is all the difference in the world between a squire's residence and a craft centre. Robert Ashwin Maynard, who figures large in the story of the Press, was sent by the sisters to learn pottery in London so as to set up this section of the craft guild, and although some pottery was made, this part of the plan was in vain. The pattern for future conferences was laid as early as January 1921 when the two sisters discussed the problems of post-war Wales with a group of friends from the Welsh School of Social Service. It included a solemn service of dedication. It was only by chance in 1924 that the two sisters went to live permanently at Gregynog. It became necessary for the family and the furniture to move temporarily out of Plas Dinam, Llandinam (a house built by the great Victorian Aesthetic architect W. E. Nesfield) for it to be redecorated for the second wife of David Davies. Mrs. Edward Davies disliked the coniferous gloom of the Gregynog estate and fully intended to take her step-daughters and their governess Miss Blaker (sister of Hugh Blaker) back to Llandinam, to live at Bron Eirion. When the time came, however, the two sisters insisted upon staying on in their craft centre, and Mrs. Davies left for Bron Eirion alone. If Miss Blaker represented a very English influence upon the sisters' lives, their stepmother, the daughter of a local farmer, and an aristocrat in Calvinistic Methodism in every way, represented their link with a more truly Welsh past. Despite their desire to set up house on their own, the two sisters were devoted to their stepmother and would visit her frequently and take her out for drives in the country in the motor car.

Gregynog in this way became permanently the home of the two sisters (although they spent a good deal of each year holidaying abroad or in their flat in London), and permanently the home of the Press; for various short periods each year the house was a conference centre, and for one long week-end, the home of the Gregynog Festival. Since a good deal

of the house was now to become a private residence again, a good deal
of building was needed to accommodate the conference members, so the
billiard room of Lord Joicey at the eastern end of the main house was
enlarged and converted into a music room, and the delicate canvases of
the French landscapists and the ecstasies of the school of El Greco
replaced the Edwardian masculinity of Joicey. To the north, between
the main house and the stables an annexe of new bedrooms was built.
The house was furnished partly with furniture from Llandinam, partly
from the flat in Buckingham Gate in London, and partly with simple
modern purchases, later supplemented by some fine furniture made by
unemployed miners at the Bryn-mawr community, in the southern
coalfield. The cushions with their embroidered Celtic interlacing, which
still remain in the house, were part of the characteristic work of the
miners' wives at Bryn-mawr.

Guests to Gregynog in the twenties, accustomed perhaps to the
cluttered, potted-palmed, gilt-and-brocade atmosphere of Edwardian
country houses, must have found it most strange, with its odd para-
doxical mixture of the grand and the spartan, the faintly carbolic school-
room air imparted by the light oak Bryn-mawr furnishings, and the
majestic paintings a riot of colour, but in styles which must have appeared
outrageous to them. This paradox arose possibly from the contrasting
tastes of the two sisters, Gwendoline the elder and more formidable with
a more conventionally upper class taste for the luxurious and fine, and
Margaret the younger and more shy, with a liking for telling simplicity
of texture and form. The gardens which they restored and extended
around the house also reflected this difference, the mixed herbaceous
borders and Victorian bedding-out, and on the other hand the shaded
and mysterious dells and dingles with their rare and exotic specimens,
all in the same garden. The sisters themselves, who welcomed guests
with great frequency to the house outside conference and festival time,
and were an odd mixture of gregarious taciturnity, must also have been
a puzzle to the more conventional visitor, since they were not conventionally aristocratic, nor conventionally plutocratic, middle class or
bohemian. To the English visitor, it was a surprise to find that the sisters
identified themselves closely with their chapel background, were fond of
welcoming ministers to their house, were strict teetotallers, and great
chapelgoers both in Llandinam and in London. Gwendoline told Dora

Herbert Jones in later years that she had in her youth spent every night of the week but one at the chapel in Llandinam, playing or practising the organ and at other chapel functions like the Band of Hope. With their concern for Welsh causes, and their frequent donations to Welsh institutions, they must have appeared profoundly Welsh to the English visitor. Their chapel background and unconventional tastes in many ways cut them off from many of the Montgomeryshire gentry, although they did have close contacts with some of the old Liberal families such as Humphreys Owen of Glansevern, who were also gentry. But the more conventional Welsh visitor must have found them a puzzle too, for they appeared to be so very un-Welsh in many ways. Their stepmother spoke good Welsh, and their brother David spoke a little, but Gwendoline hardly spoke or understood any, while to Margaret Welsh was quite foreign. By upper class English standards life at Gregynog was very simple, there was a butler for a short time, and a number of servants naturally in so large a house, but none of the liveried footmen one might expect. But for Welsh delegates coming to conferences to discuss the future of the Sunday school in Wales, or the tragedy of the miners, Gregynog was the very lap of luxury, and the sisters despite their deep concern for things Welsh, appeared grandly upper class, cushioned by wealth against the Depression.

During the early twenties, then, Gregynog became for the first time in its history celebrated, partly by the work of the Press, and partly by the work of its conferences. The sisters had arrived at a time of crisis. 'In the time of prosperity, rejoice; in the time of adversity, consider' says the Old Testament. The conferences had begun in 1921 as small affairs, sometimes no more than musical retreats for Aberystwyth college students. From 1921 to 1938 a number of organizations met for their annual conferences at Gregynog: the Welsh School of Social Service; the League of Nations Union Advisory Educational Committee; and the National Council of Music for Wales, for example. But as the twenties became more grey than gay, and the Welsh crisis deepened into tragedy, the conferences dealt more and more with the social problems of the coalfield, for example the Distressed Areas Conferences from 1920 to 1937. It was the Davies family who built the Temple of Peace and Health in Cathays Park, Cardiff, in order to provide in the metropolis a centre which would achieve on a large scale what was done on a small scale at Gregynog.

Some things were achieved by these conferences, the patronage of Bryn Mawr and other similar communities in the valleys did alleviate a little suffering here and there, the organisation of children's holiday camps as at Boverton did the same, but little profound change could be achieved in conferences to discuss the world. The atmosphere of the conferences was rather like a school, earnest, simple, well-organised, methodical, moralistic, high-minded. Larger meetings were held in the Music Room, and smaller less formal meetings all around the house. Informal services were held on Sunday mornings so that members did not avoid religious devotions simply because the various places of worship were a long way from the house, and these house services were the kernel of the much more elaborate festival services of 1934 to 1938. It is very easy to sneer at those conferences, and to say that they achieved little. But Wales had no centre for conferences or discussions of this kind, which every nation should have in its capital as a matter of course, and the Gregynog meetings between the wars were an important part of that process by which we have changed from the Victorian situation when any meeting of any importance for Wales was held in London, and they prepared the way for a great spread of committees and boards for discussing things Welsh which have arisen since the Second World War. A prophetic conference in this respect was the stormy one organised in 1937, to which Sir John Reith was invited, on the future of broadcasting in Wales.

From 1934 until 1938 for one long week-end in the Summer, Gregynog was the home of a music festival which made its name famous in circles who knew little of the Welsh Council of Social Service. As for the conferences, the house was filled with fuss and flurry, the sisters and their staff spent many nervous weeks planning beforehand, not only preparing rooms and food, for·the forty or so house guests and artistes, but the Davies sisters and most of their staff formed a unique house choir which sang during the festivals. It was the only time of the year when Gregynog resembled a conventionally aristocratic country house, for guests took dinner in full fig, and during the day strolled through the grounds or played tennis in white flannels. But the paradox is apparent here: the two sisters lived shut away in a great house surrounded by a vast park, and yet they both never missed a weekly choir practice, singing 'in the ranks' on a par with their humblest servants, as though they were symbols of the *Gwerin* democracy of the Land of Song. The Festivals were a time of gaiety and laughter. The guests were carefully chosen, sometimes family friends, sometimes celebrities brought by Thomas Jones such as George Bernard Shaw or Helen Waddell. Their intellectual tastes were anticipated, and guests were often surprised to find the very books which suited them in their bedrooms. Apparently the only guest who was openly allowed alcohol at Gregynog was Stanley Baldwin, the Prime Minister, who is said to have convinced the two sisters that he needed it for his health. For the concerts there would be about seventy people in all in the Music Room, with forty or so staying in the house. It was undoubtedly the zenith of the year at Gregynog. The festival services were prepared with great care, and for many of the guests were the high point of the festival. But these solemn ceremonies, conducted with tact and taste, were only a part of the festival, for the guests also joined in more merry and jolly sing-songs when they got the opportunity. Bernard Shaw would entertain them in the drawing room by reading his own plays, himself acting all the parts, or perhaps guests would join with Sir Walford Davies in some grotesque mock-Victorian oratorio. For those who lived in and around Gregynog, the festivals were something to look forward to, to work for, and to look back at with nostalgia. They were the other side of the coin from the earnest conferences, and they were the alternative aspect of the gloomy years of the Depression.

This has brought us a very long way from William Morris. A hostile observer might condemn the whole Gregynog venture between the wars as rootless, affected and vain, and worse than that, a kind of fiddling while Rome was burning. But it should be seen as part of a much larger frame of activities of the Davies family in the 1920s and 30s to transform the life of Wales embracing all kinds of things, craft guilds, a new secular but moralistic magazine *The Welsh Outlook*, conference centres such as the Temple of Peace, children's summer camps, boards of music, a new national art collection, sanatoria and hospitals, all kinds of schemes of which Gregynog was only a tiny part. It is astonishing at first sight to see the family lavishing their thousands on these projects at a time of economic disaster when the sources of their wealth, coal and railways, appeared to be drying up, although we may find outside life and in literature families which offer some parallel to this change, such as the Buddenbrooks or the Forsytes. Whenever one looks for parallels or explanations by comparisons, one returns to the simple fact that Gregynog under the Davieses was unique. It is not an historian's question in the least, but one wonders what would have happened if William Morris had been born a little later, and had been sent by Thomas Jones up to Gregynog to manage the community there. It would have been a great adventure.*

* The domestic and biographical details of this short memoir come from conversations recorded with Dora Herbert Jones shortly before her death. Gregynog MSS. also contain some short memoranda on conferences and meetings at Gregynog from 1921 onwards by T. W. Hughes.

CHAPTER SIX

MUSIC IN GREGYNOG

JOHN HYWEL

'The home of Gwendoline and Margaret Davies is unique among country houses in Wales and I know of no parallel in England'.[1]

To understand the quality of life that made this country house unique, particularly during the years between the World Wars, it is necessary to understand something of its owners, Miss Gwendoline Davies and Miss Margaret (Daisy) Davies, together with two of their closest friends, Dr. Thomas Jones (the writer of the opening quotation), and Sir Walford Davies.

Gwendoline and Margaret Davies were very well educated. They went to an exclusive boarding school in Hendon, and had Miss Jane Blaker, a most outstanding personality, as governess. They also travelled extensively, Mrs. Edward Davies, their stepmother, being a firm believer in this method of absorbing the cultural heritage of the many countries they visited. They were encouraged to develop their talents, Gwendoline in music, and Margaret in painting. Gwendoline the elder and more dominant sister, was trained as a violinist and an organist. She owned a Stradivarius (the 'Parke'), and became a competent player, until a rare blood disease forced her to give up playing in her middle twenties. As an organist, she played for services at the local chapel and, to very close friends only, on the Gregynog organ. A very well-read woman, she was particularly interested in religious prose and poetry. Religion, or rather organised religion, had always meant a great deal to the Davies family, they were all faithful Presbyterians and regularly worshipped at the local church. Margaret was always interested in painting, her greatest delight being the painting of flowers.

Cultured, widely travelled, artistic, religious. Add to all this an element of shyness and some general idea of the Misses Davies will emerge. It must be realised that two unmarried sisters would not enjoy such freedom of action in the strict convention of the early 1900s as they would today.

---

[1] Thomas Jones, *Welsh Broth* (London 1950), p. 168.

They were not at all at home in crowds of strangers, and yet, at the same time were keen to enjoy company outside the immediate family. Having plenty of money and a lovely home, it seemed only natural to invite a number of people there to enjoy the things that they enjoyed, music, poetry, paintings and the beautiful gardens. But in no sense was Gregynog to become a 'Shangri-la', cut off and escaping from the harsh realities of life by immersion in great art. The sisters, true to the family tradition, were much concerned with the world outside, and by opening their house to conferences on musical and social matters and international affairs, contributed a great deal to numerous causes.

An early idea had been to make Gregynog a craft centre, in fact some pottery was made there in the early twenties, but the decision by the sisters to make Gregynog their permanent home meant the abandonment of that scheme. Thomas Jones began his long association with the Davies family in 1910 when he became Secretary to the King Edward VII Welsh National Memorial Association. For over forty years he was to be counsellor and friend to the sisters, and it was he who first introduced the sisters to Dr. Walford Davies. They met in 1918 at a lunch 'the object of which was to induce Dr. Walford, at the age of forty-nine, to leave the Temple and its famous choir and settle in Wales'.[2] The enticement was the double appointment as first Director of the newly formed Council of Music for Wales, and first Gregynog Professor of Music at Aberystwyth. A large anonymous donation from the sisters had greatly assisted the setting up of both Council and Chair, and so it was right that they should have some say in this appointment. Dr. Walford yielded to their tender persuasion and accepted the position. He was soon to become a close friend of the sisters and, like Tom Jones, a frequent visitor at their home.

Walford Davies and 'Music in Gregynog' are inseparable. He was the moving spirit behind the musical developments of the next twenty years. A musician of the highest quality, imbued with immense vitality, he was also a humble and a deeply religious man, having 'the heart of a child and a simple deep child-like faith that flowed into all he did and which was the true source of all his strength and appeal'.[3] Gwendoline Davies, Walford Davies and Dora Herbert Jones[4] shared a great interest in

[2] Thomas Jones, *Leeks and Daffodils* (Newtown 1942), p. 169.
[3] A friend of Walford Davies's, quoted by Thomas Jones in *Leeks and Daffodils*, p. 177.
[4] The well known singer and interpreter of folk songs, who was secretary to the Gregynog Press from 1927 until its closure in 1939–40, remaining as Gwendoline Davies's private secretary until 1942.

devotional literature and this, allied to Walford Davies's expertise and experience with religious services was to influence considerably the future course of events.

Religious services were held at Gregynog from the very start. With all the conferences taking place over long week-ends, the Misses Davies did not like the idea that delegates would miss church on the Sunday. Since members of different denominations would have to separate and travel some distance to their respective places of worship, thus effectively breaking up the conference for the whole of the Sunday morning, the sisters decided to hold inter-denominational services in the house. These were usually held from ten till eleven, with conference sessions resuming immediately afterwards. The house was never consecrated, which meant that Roman Catholics were free to attend the services without the necessity of a special dispensation. The first record in the Visitors book is of a Service of Dedication held at 4 p.m. on Saturday, 15 January 1921, during a weekend when the Education Group of the Welsh School of Social Service was meeting at Gregynog. This service took place in the dining room, since there was not yet a hall of any description in the house, two local ministers took part, and brief addresses were given by Thomas Jones, Percy E. Watkins[5] and Herbert Morgan.[6] Two hymns were sung to piano accompaniment, 'When wilt Thou save the People', and 'These things shall be'. The words of this great hymn could well stand as a motto for the spirit of Gregynog as it was to develop,

New arts shall bloom of loftier mould,
And mightier music thrill the skies,
And ev'ry life shall be a song,
When all the earth is paradise.

The pattern was therefore established, the services taking place in the dining room, in the drawing room, in the open air, and later in the music room when this was added to the house. The make-up of the individual service depended to a considerable extent on the nature of the conference, so that not only would suitable and meaningful prayers and readings be chosen, but sometimes music by the great masters might be played by musicians attending the particular conference. At the 1921 Council of Music service 'the instruments joined in Bach's "Wachet Auf" ' (Walford's

---

[5] Permanent Secretary, Welsh Department, Board of Education.
[6] Minister and Director of Extra Mural Studies, U.C.W. Aberystwyth.

signature tune!); at a retreat of music students and staff-members from the music department of U.C.W. in the same year 'the slow movement from Beethoven's "Archduke" was played'.

The early entries in the visitors' book record mostly meetings of musicians, in 1921 the second annual conference of the National Council of Music in July, and the Aberystwyth Music Department Retreat in late October. 1922 saw a working party staying a week to complete the School and College Hymnal for the printer, and the Council of Music's Third Annual Conference. Gradually the spectrum of activity widens, with meetings later that year of the Montgomeryshire County Nursing Association, the Advisory Education Committee of the League of Nations—this movement being close to the heart of David Davies, later Lord Davies, the Education Group of the Welsh School of Social Service and the Welsh Schoolboys Camp Movement. This by no means gives a comprehensive list of the groups who were to attend often annual re-unions at Gregynog for the next twenty years, but does give some idea of the general pattern of activity in the house. It is important to realise clearly that Gregynog was not a 'conference centre' in the way it is today, when groups representing many different bodies may visit Gregynog on application. Every person visiting Gregynog was an invited guest of the sisters, and so the organisations represented were those with which the sisters were strongly in sympathy. As guests of the sisters, conference members naturally respected the wishes of their hosts, and two things in particular were memorable, the beautiful services, and the fact that no alcohol was ever allowed. The sisters were true Presbyterians of their time!

'Walford was the music of this place—and everything that came, came in his style.'[7] This was true, and it is equally true to say that wherever you found Walford Davies, there you would also find music. He was no academic, talking about music in a vacuum, he made music and inspired others with his enthusiasm and ideals to make music themselves. As Director of the Council of Music, he thought it important that there should be music taking place at the same time as the annual meetings of the Council, which were held at Gregynog from 1921 to 1938. Council members should hear, as well as discuss, music. In 1921, 'many worshippers

[7] Dora Herbert Jones.

from both churches in Tregynon came on Sunday evening to hear and join in music by Bach, Beethoven, Wesley, and in Welsh melody'. In 1923, a chorus of delegates from the Montgomeryshire Festival Choirs, an orchestra from Aberystwyth, Bangor and Cardiff Colleges with Charles Clements at the organ and John Morgan Nicholas at the piano gave a performance of the St. Matthew Passion, conducted by Walford Davies. The edition of the work had been specially prepared by the Council (in sol-fa and old notation), and the soloists included the famous soprano Madame Laura Evans-Williams, Miss Dilys Jones, Mr. Tom Pickering and Mr. W. R. Allen. This was the first large scale performance of anything at Gregynog, and took place in the new Hall or Music Room as it was called, in which was installed a fine organ.

Previously the Music Room had been a billiards room, and any music making took place in the library, the drawing room, or even the open air. As time went on, it was realised that a proper hall where more formal concerts could be held was necessary, and so the billiards room was extended by adding a stage and installing an organ at the back of this stage. In fact considerable alterations were made to the house in general at this time, the Annexe being added so as to increase the number of bedrooms. Walford Davies naturally had considerable say in planning the new Hall, the work being carried out and supervised by Mr. T. W. Hughes, who remained at Gregynog as estate manager. The organ was built by Frederick Rothwell, in close consultation with Walford Davies. It grew in three distinct stages, a small two-manual, becoming a large two-manual and finally a three-manual instrument by 1925. It occasionally got low on wind pressure, perhaps because it had been augmented from the original small two-manual instrument, but it nevertheless possessed a remarkable tone quality, particularly in the softer stops, which transported the listener 'to the edge of silence'. There were some expressive solo stops, the visitors' book of July 1926 recording 'The new stop on the organ—a perfect clarinet by Rothwell—was greatly enjoyed, and seems to set a new standard onto the minds of us all for organ reeds.' This organ was the fourth out of five that Rothwell and Walford Davies were jointly concerned with, the first three being in London churches where Walford Davies had held posts and the last to be the famous twin console instrument at St. George's, Windsor, where he served as organist from 1927–32.

It is quite wrong to imagine that the organ was built solely for use in services and concerts at the behest of Walford Davies. Gwendoline Davies was an organist in her own right, and the Gregynog organ was built equally for her enjoyment. She loved to spend an hour playing this fine instrument, 'though her shyness forbade her play to an audience of more than one or two close friends. Her secretary and librarian, Dora Herbert Jones, was often asked to join her in the hall whilst she played, a favourite piece being 'He shall feed his flock', with Dora singing to Gwen's accompaniment.

The deliberations, very often fiery and intolerant of the Council of Music, were naturally of considerable importance to the musical life of the Principality, but it is easy to underestimate the importance of the musical performances at these Conferences. The latest Council venture could be paraded for all to hear, and judge its value. Thus, on several occasions, the instrumental trios of Aberystwyth, Bangor and Cardiff played individually, and joined together to form a chamber orchestra. In 1924 a contingent of the new Welsh Symphony Orchestra played overtures, Haydn's 'Clock' Symphony and accompanied Miss Sybil Eaton in Brahms' violin concerto. It was rare indeed to hear any music by Welsh composers, String Quartet music on folk songs by E. T. Davies and Hubert Davies, and songs by Vaughan Thomas being among the few examples performed during conferences. In those days Welsh music was considered of inferior quality, a view strongly held by both Walford Davies and the sisters.

One can quite clearly express the musical life of Gregynog in four periods:

(i) 1921–28 Ad hoc services, Council of Music concerts, informal music making (Christmas parties, student retreats), and concerts given by staff and students from Aberystwyth, whilst Walford Davies was professor. He resigned in 1927, and there is no record of a formal concert between 1926 and 1929 (apart from those connected with the Council of Music).[8]

(ii) 1929–32 With the formation of the Gregynog Choir, annual concerts of choral music are held every April.

(iii) 1933–8 The six Festivals of Music and Poetry.

(iv) 1939–52 War, and the death of Sir Walford, put an end to all music.

---

[8] Due to heart trouble in 1926, Walford Davies resigned the Chair at Aberystwyth to David de Lloyd, though retaining the general Directorship of the National Council of Music.

In 1954, after a lapse of fifteen years, Professor Ian Parrott brought music back to the house, putting on a series of one-concert Festivals from 1956 to 1961.

Music making at Gregynog was by no means always a solemn and formal affair, for Walford was a joyful and exuberant personality. In April 1922, during the meeting of the Aberystwyth working party on the hymnal 'a short concert was given in the evening to a few visitors in which all present were induced to join in one way or another. Everyone sang the chorus songs "Upidee", "Will ye no come back again", and "Green grow the rushes"!' Many happy after-Christmas parties are recorded when local choristers and musicians from Aberystwyth gave concerts of Christmas Music to the house guests and neighbouring friends of the Misses Davies. 1924 was a most ambitious programme, carols being followed by Parts I and II of Bach's 'Christmas Oratorio'. A grateful house-guest writes 'No doubt Gregynog, the house itself has by now got a spirit, a personality of its own. We, who were guests—we go back to our workaday life, saying what a house wonderful is Gregynog, and what a winter debt we owe to our hostesses—the three ladies of Gregynog.'[9]

Other events of musical interest during this first period include the famous Musical Mission of 1923, when Walford and the boys of the Temple Choir spent ten hectic days at Gregynog, preparing for their tour around the churches and halls of Wales in an effort to propagate the gospel of music. Walford and his Aberystwyth contingent gave two October concerts in 1925 and 1926, and there were several meetings in the house of the conductors of Montgomeryshire choirs, when Walford expounded the delights and the problems of the 'St. Matthew Passion', 'Judas Maccabeus', or whatever was the chosen Festival work.

The first record of the Gregynog choir appears in 1929 when, during a meeting on the distressed areas of South Wales, 'The Gregynog choir, led by Allen, sang Bach's "Jesu, Priceless Treasure" and Walford's "Lord, it belongs not to my care"—a glorious ending to a perfect day.'

By 1929, after eight years of increasing music-making and increasing numbers of conferences with their Sunday morning services, with an acoustically fine hall and a pure-toned organ, with Gwendoline and

---

[9] The third lady was Mrs. Edward Davies, who lived at Gregynog whilst Plas Dinam was undergoing extensive alterations.

Margaret Davies keen singers and Dora Herbert Jones an outstanding soloist, and, above all else, with Sir Walford[10] as a regular visitor, the formation of a house-choir seemed inevitable. Several choirs had performed in Gregynog, the Aberystwyth Small Choir (1925), the English Singers (1927), and delegates from local choirs, so it was known that the facilities were adequate for choral singing. Henry Breeze, the *codwr canu* in the local chapel ran a village choir anyway, so there was a nucleus near at hand, and Walford's enthusiasm and expertise were guaranteed to raise the necessary recruits. This was a true house-choir, since a large number of the male choristers worked in the house, for the Press or on the estate, some of their wives sang, and of course Dora and the Misses Davies were leading members. The legendary tale of advertising for a gardener with a strong tenor voice is a complete myth, although there was one classic case of a man being appointed because he was a *codwr canu* with a marvellous natural voice. No doubt he was also proficient at his trade.

The house-choir came to number about twenty-eight, this number being augmented to forty for the Festivals and other big occasions. They rehearsed for two hours every Friday through the year from September to July. W. R. Allen travelled from Aberystwyth to teach them the notes and do the initial training, so that they would be fully prepared when Walford or Adrian Boult came to add polish and an interpretation to the performance. When one knows the extensive and most demanding repertoire that this choir tackled in the years 1929–39, it is easy to forget that these were for the most part just ordinary country choralists, and not trained London singers. Most of the women and three of the men understood old-notation, most of the men read sol-fa but some read nothing at all and learnt the music by ear. Dora's sister Gertrude Rowlands spent many arduous hours transcribing into sol-fa, and where works like Holst's 'Grecian Urn' are involved this is a labour of extreme difficulty, for key changes (a permanent head-ache to sol-fa'ists) are constant and often unusual. It is a very great tribute to Allen that he managed to teach this repertoire to a choir of ordinary folk, whose previous musical experience would have been slight.

The choir was a house-choir in all senses, and always rehearsed and performed in the Music Room. The full forty-voice Festival Choir was

---

[10] Dr. Walford Davies was knighted in 1922, for his services to music at the Temple Church.

arranged on the stage in two groups of twenty, Choir I's five sopranos, five altos, five tenors and five basses complemented by the same numbers in Choir II on the other side of the stage, with a gangway between them for Charles Clements to find his way to the organ stool. Each section had its leaders, amongst whom were Dora (first soprano), Gwendoline (first alto), and Margaret (second soprano). This division into double-choir with eight real parts, was absolutely necessary in view of the music they were to sing, the traditional Welsh four-part choir being quite unsuitable for the Vaughan-Williams Mass (double-choir) or the Byrd five part Mass. As appearance was considered as important as sound, Gwendoline supplied all the ladies with long light dresses in deep ecru —all fitted individually, and the men wore dark lounge suits with black bow ties.

The repertoire was daunting, the Matthew Passion, Holst's 'Grecian Urn', Vaughan Williams's 'Mass in G minor' and Byrd's 'Mass for Five Voices' forming but a small part. They were but local singers. And yet, even today, unbiased visitors to those pre-war concerts recall the choir in terms of glowing admiration, and the visitors' book waxes ecstatic with praise. How was such a standard achieved, a standard which satisfied such men as Gustav Holst and Ralph Vaughan-Williams? The answer must lie in the genius, yes, the genius of Walford Davies. Thomas Jones writes 'Perhaps it was as a choir-trainer that Sir Walford was at his best. He made the simplest country singers rich with the wealth of the great composers, shared out amongst them by waving his magical wand.' Charles Clements mentions Walford's acute ear, seeking out a soft yet rich uniform production of tone from all his singers, stressing particularly a crystal clear enunciation based firmly on a clear understanding of the meaning of the words. 'Sing listeningly' was one of his favourite expressions, encouraging soft tone and an awareness of what the other choral parts were doing. Deeply religious, he was at his greatest in directing Psalms, exhorting the Choir to 'sing as fast as you can and as slow as you must!' One of his greatest rhetorical gifts was that of pictorial imagery, and this was brought into full play in his contacts with the country people of Wales, a people acquainted with and highly responsive to the imagery found in the wealth of 'stories' that formed the stock-in-trade of every successful nonconformist preacher.

If Walford provided inspiration, Adrian Boult added interpretation. He first visited Gregynog in May 1925, it being the custom for the conductor and soloists at the newly formed Montgomeryshire Festival to stay in Gregynog over the Festival period. In this way Elsie Suddaby, Keith Faulkner and others, were to begin their friendship with the sisters—who were of course the patrons of the Festival, with Walford Davies as overall artistic director. Adrian Boult actually conducted one Gregynog concert in October 1925, but his regular appearances there did not begin until April 1930, with the first Matthew Passion that the Gregynog choir was to take part in, aided at this time by delegates from nearby choirs, since it was not yet of sufficient strength or experience to tackle this great work unaided.

A concert held every April, near to the Easter period, became the main annual musical event in the years 1929–32, and these can clearly be seen, together with the elaborate services at the larger conferences, as fore-runners of the Festivals of Music and Poetry of 1933–8. Gradually standards and ideals rose higher. The Aberystwyth-based contingent of musicians (Walford's friends from his time as Professor), were joined more and more by artists of national repute from London (more friends of Walford). In the 1932 concert, the 'home-team' of Sir Walford Davies, Miss Evelyn Cooke, Mr. W. R. Allen and Mr. Charles Clements were joined by Miss Elsie Suddaby, Mr. Adrian Boult and Dr. Ralph Vaughan-Williams. The choir's repertoire was rapidly increasing, Madrigals, Folk-songs and Vaughan-Williams's 'Mass in G minor' (1931) being followed by 'How Lovely are thy dwellings' from Brahms's 'Requiem', and Vaughan-Williams's 'Benedicite' in 1932. Some of the music from the April concerts would be repeated in July for the benefit of delegates to the Council of Music conferences.

*   *   *   *

'A memory we shall all treasure will be that of the exquisite singing in the service in the music room' (October 1931).

'The service on Sunday was deeply helpful to us and wholly beautiful' (July 1933).

'We were unspeakably grateful for the consolation and purification of spirit which we experienced at the Sunday morning service' (September 1938).

Again and again such comments are recorded in the visitors' book. There is no question but that these services made a wholly unforgettable impression on the congregations in the Music Room in the 1930s. Before this the services were fairly brief affairs—planned partly by the minister, partly by general discussion with the sisters, Dora and Walford, to be typed out simply on a single copy for the minister's use.

In September 1930, through the influence of Lord Davies and Thomas Jones, the International Conference of the Burge Memorial Trust was held at Gregynog. The guests were people of great influence and importance in France, Germany, and Great Britain. It was felt by Gwendoline and Dora that the foreign visitors would not understand much of the Sunday morning service unless they had the text in front of them, so it was decided to plan the service down to the last detail, and have it printed by the Gregynog Press. The service was very freely based on the services of the Church of England, with prayers and lessons chosen suitable to the ideals of the Burge Trust. It built up to a Litany of Commemoration, the poignant words enhanced by the red poppies placed in front of the El Greco screen standing at the front of the stage. As a conclusion, a part of Mendelssohn's 'Hymn of Praise' was sung as a tribute to one of the guests, Dr. Albrecht Mendelssohn-Bartholdy, the grandson of the composer.

The pattern was set. Printed services now appear for all major conferences, four of which recur from year to year—Social Reconstruction in the Distressed Areas of South Wales in January, the National Council of Music in July, the Advisory Education Committee of the League of Nations Union in November, and the South Wales Girls' Camp in December. Note the personal interest of the sisters in each of these, two concerning South Wales whence came the family fortune and where the family always laboured to alleviate the lot of the poor, the League of Nations through their brother, and the Council of Music.

Although each service was planned separately with a theme chosen relevant to the conference and sometimes the season of the Christian year, nevertheless the initial format, once established by the Burge Trust service was not to be radically altered. Everything was chosen beforehand, the place of the address or sermon being taken by readings selected from the finest devotional and philosophical prose and poetry. These include extracts from the Book of Wisdom, Pericles, Plato, Lincoln, Gilbert

Murray, Oliver Lodge, Eliot, Lionel Curtis, and Lascelles Abercrombie. The four 'Distressed Areas' Services of 1932–5 develop even further by the inclusion of extended meditations in prose and poetry, in which the minister, a reader, sometimes called simply 'Poet', Cantor and Choir take part. Prayers would be drawn from many sources in addition to the Book of Common Prayer, and several Litanies were used.

The separate parts of the Service were clearly indicated, thus 'An Act of Remembrance', 'Litany of the League', 'Remembrance and Dedication'. Gwendoline Davies and Dora Herbert Jones spent a very great deal of time planning the services, with some expert assistance from Lascelles Abercrombie, a poet of distinction, who was Professor of English Literature at Bedford College, London.

Musically, the influence of Walford Davies was paramount. Although for the most part drawn from introits, anthems, sections of the Mass, psalms and hymns that one might hear in a Cathedral Church, occasionally the music came from a wider sphere, such as 'Ye now are sorrowful' and 'How lovely are thy dwellings' from Brahms's Requiem, and parts of Vaughan-Williams's 'Dona Nobis Pacem'. Introits and anthems included 'Thou wilt keep him' and 'Lead me Lord' (Wesley), 'King of Glory' and 'Jesu Joy of man's desiring' (Bach), 'To my humble supplication' (Holst), and four by Walford Davies himself, 'O Emmanuel Rex', 'God be in my head', 'Blessed are the Pure in heart' and 'Lord, it belongs not to my care'. The 'Agnus Dei' and 'Gloria' as set by Vaughan-Williams, and Bach chorales 'Jesu priceless treasure' and the favourite 'Wachet Auf' ('Zion hear the watchmen's voices') appeared, together with interludes of organ music and the 'Beatitudes' of Elgar. The psalms were a particular glory, as interpreted by Walford, and mainly set to his own Chants, the most popular being Psalm 121, 'I will lift up mine eyes unto the hills; from whence cometh my help'. Many well-known hymns were used, two of these recurring regularly, 'These things shall be', and the Battle hymn of the Republic—'Mine eyes have seen the glory'. Nor was the wealth of emotive Welsh hymnology ignored, with the presence of 'Braint', 'O Iesu mawr' and 'Dysg fi fy Nuw, dysg fi pa fodd', sometimes played by a single 'cello, sometimes sung solo, and sometimes sung by the congregation, with a free English translation printed beneath the Welsh text.

Relatives and neighbouring friends would join the forty or so conference members, making a congregation of some sixty to seventy in all.
Gwendoline Davies would invite people to take part in the Service,
Thomas Jones, Ben Bowen Thomas, Alun Oldfield Davies and, most
often, Lascelles Abercrombie among them. They took the prayers and
generally led the devotions, with the Gregynog house-choir half-hidden
behind the El Greco, accompanied by Charles Clements on the organ,
singing the psalms and introits, the congregation only joining in the
hymns. Normally, W. R. Allen directed the choir, but on the more
special occasions Walford Davies and Adrian Boult would be present.
Solo singers took part but rarely, and it is Miss Elsie Suddaby's singing
of 'Ye now are sorrowful' which remains in people's memories. The
printed service was totally explanatory, 'The congregation is requested
to stand during the prayers and to join in the hymns, responses and
prayers which are printed in italics,' this lack of verbal directives to 'stand'
and 'sit' greatly adding to the devotional atmosphere.

The impact of these Services was very considerable. The Gregynog
Service was unique in conception and near-perfect in execution. Nothing
in our earthly existence can be wholly perfect, but the beauty and
spirituality of the greatest literature and music combined into a single
Act of Devotion and Worship, taking place in a room hung with paintings
by Turner, Constable, Monet and Millet, all dominated by the El Greco
hung on a screen, must be as close to that unattainable perfection as we
can ever hope to reach. All who attended went away with an added
strength of purpose, and the awareness of total beauty in great art placed
the evils and sometimes petty annoyances they were combating into a
truer perspective.

'To be at the service was to realise the truth of the word of the writer
of Ecclesiastes "He hath made everything delightful in its order; He
hath set eternity in their hearts".' (November 1931).

*   *   *   *

The first mention of a Festival occurs in the visitors' book during a
visit by Walford and his wife Margaret in September 1932, ' "Gregynog
Festival" seen clearly on the horizon for the first time.

> "Our dream shall become their present
> And their work in this world be done" '.

The events of their first twelve years at Gregynog can clearly be seen, artistically speaking, as leading towards these Festivals. The development of the Services, with their integration of music and poetry, the close friendships with Walford Davies and Lascelles Abercrombie, the growing number of fine musicians who regularly visit the house, all these factors combine in influencing the decision to hold a Festival.

Six Festivals of Music and Poetry were to be held in the Music Room at Gregynog between 1933 and 1938. They always took place in late June or early July, when the gardens were at their best, the weather was warm, and it remained light until late evening, so that the guests and artists could stroll through the grounds before and after the evening concerts. Every member of the audience was a guest of the Misses Davies, forty or so staying in the house, many more in local hotels, their bills paid by the sisters, and perhaps a hundred or more travelling in from their homes for every concert. A guest at the house would discover the beautifully printed Festival Programme on arrival in his bedroom, containing complete details and text of all the music, with the poetry either unspecified, the titles given, or else the full text supplied, the planners' ideas changing over the years. The musicians appearing in the concerts took their places as guests in the house. They were not just any old hard-bitten professionals, they were there because of their interest in Gregynog and what it stood for, being highly cultured people themselves believing firmly in the ideals of Gwendoline and Margaret Davies. Musicians were certainly paid for their services, but this was not the reason why they returned to Gregynog year after year.

The roll-call of artists is an impressive one. Sir Walford and Adrian Boult conducted the choir and a string orchestra of some twelve members, made up of chamber music players, who thus fulfilled a dual role at the Festivals. Most of the players were known to Walford at Aberystwyth and through his work for the Council of Music, but a few came from further afield. Violinists included the fabled Jelly d'Aranyi on one occasion, W. H. Reed—the friend of Elgar, and the composer Hubert Davies, with his wife Hannah as violist. Amongst the 'cellists was Arthur Williams, one of the finest interpreters of chamber music of his generation. In 1935 came the renowned Rothschild Quartet. Guests wandering around the house and grounds were able to hear these artists at work, and it is recalled that 'the rehearsal of Schubert's "Quintet on Monday" with Jelly d'Aranyi and Arthur Williams was a marvellous joy'. In the final festival the name Eldrydd Dugdale appears as 'cellist. She was later to marry 'Mike' Davies, Lord Davies's son, a keen amateur musician who gained tremendous pleasure from the music-making in this house.

A full-sized symphony orchestra would have been entirely out of place in the small and intimate concert hall, so Charles Clements had the task of 'filling-in' all the missing parts on the organ. Walford sometimes added piano to the ensemble so the orchestra for the fully scored choral works of Elgar, Brahms and Vaughan-Williams would at most comprise six violins, three violas, three 'cellos, piano and organ. In the fairly dry acoustic of the music room, with a choir of forty and the audience of necessity very close to the performers, the small orchestra provided by far the best solution, especially with musicians of the calibre of Clements and Walford Davies adding in all the missing woodwind and brass parts. The orchestra was however dispensed with for the last two Festivals, the organ accompanying the choir in the larger works, and George Thalben-Ball, successor to Walford Davies and organist of the Temple Church to this day, coming and playing a number of demanding organ solos. It is recorded 'that the absence of orchestra gave us the presence of Thalben-Ball and a hearing for the first time of the beauties and vast potentialities of "Daddy" Rothwell's beautiful organ'.

The solo singers were all of the highest class, Elsie Suddaby, Mary Jarred and Keith Faulkner becoming regulars, with Tom Pickering and W. R. Allen the only remaining representatives of the former Aberystwyth contingent. The great Leila Megane came once, but apparently did not go down at all well with the highly sophisticated Gregynog audience, since her performance is tactfully unmentioned in the visitors' book.

Five people only were to appear as Readers, Lascelles Abercrombie, Ellen Bowick—the sisters' elocution teacher, Helen Waddell, Z. Havercroft Jones and Robert Speaight. These were all fine speakers—though none approached Abercrombie for the ability to captivate an audience with the spoken word. These readers had to be fine actors, for poetry readings were a most uncommon thing at that time, and, unlike music, a genre unfamiliar to the vast majority of the audience.

To attempt here to catalogue the music and poetry performed at the Six Festivals would be futile, since there were in all twenty-eight concerts and services. The music was written for many different media, comprising soloists, choir and orchestra, choir and organ, unaccompanied choir, solo song, string orchestra, chamber groups of every description, solo piano and solo organ. A totally random selection from the many hundreds of works reveals songs by Warlock and Dunhill, poetry by T. E. Brown, Lawrence Binyon, Edward Thomas, Walter de la Mare, Impromptu in G flat (Chopin), 'Eine Kleine Nachtmusik' (Mozart), 'Three Jovial Huntsmen' (Walford Davies), Sonata da Camera (Corelli), Concerto in C (Vivaldi), songs from Dichterliebe (Schumann), Quartet in F (Ravel), Milton's 'Samson Agonistes', 'Songs of the Fleet' (Stanford), poems by Kipling, Chesterton, Housman, St. Paul's Suite (Holst), Motet 'Sing ye to the Lord' (Bach), organ solos by Karg-Elert, Stanley, Boëllman, Welsh Airs for piano, viola and 'cello (Arwel Hughes), and the sermon from Eliot's 'Murder in the Cathedral'.

Individual concerts, rather than complete festivals, were conceived sometimes with a particular theme in mind, as the concert *in memoriam* Edward Elgar and Gustav Holst of 1934, and the always religious aspect of the Sunday evening concerts. Certain works recur, being no doubt favourites of the sisters, Parry's 'Blest Pair of Sirens', Holst's 'O Spiritual Pilgrim' (written especially for Gregynog), Elgar's 'The Music Makers' amongst these. In 1935 a chronological format was devised, Tudor and Stuart Music leading to the twentieth century by the final concert. Usually music and verse of all centuries and for many media were fitted together, the concerts bearing such titles as 'Choral and Instrumental Music and Songs', and 'Poetry, Songs and Chamber Music'. Although the aim of Gwendoline Davies in combining Music and Poetry was to achieve a Union of Equals—neither the one nor the other predominating, in actual fact Music nearly always assumed the major role and the difficulties of marrying the two Arts sometimes caused real problems, for planners, performers and audiences alike. This theme is constantly returned to in the visitors' book, 'our best success at their reconcilement seemed to reveal how vast a region there is yet to explore in which they can enhance each other without any trace of violence or disparity' (1933).

'As the claim of both become intensified, the difficulties of reconcilement in actual utterance become more wonderfully real and interesting' (1934).

An example of the union of the sister arts is the programme of Sunday, 17 June 1934.

Hymn: Caerllyngoed	
Intercession	*Holst*
Aria from Cantata 92	*Bach*
Poem: Love made me welcome	*George Herbert*
Mass in G minor	*Vaughan-Williams*
Poem: My soul, there is a Countrie	*Henry Vaughan*
Two Biblical Songs	*Dvořák*
Aria from Cantata 82	*Bach*
Aria and Chorus from 'Elijah'	*Mendelssohn*
Chorale: 'Zion hears her watchmen's voices'	*Bach*

The poetry centred on devotional verse, but war-poems by Sassoon and others began to appear as the European political situation grew ever darker. The greatest delight was to hear Abercrombie reading his own poetry, to see the actual poet alive and well was a thing of wonder. Wales was by no means forgotten, with Dora Herbert Jones singing and telling the stories of our folk-songs.

The Festival Services generally contained more music than the average conference service, reaching a high point in the concluding meditation in music and poetry, as in 1934, when part of 'Gerontius' was sung in memory of Elgar. Perhaps the most moving event of all, came in 1935, the brief morning service leading directly into Part one of the 'St. Matthew Passion', the strings beginning to play as Helen Waddell concluded the words of Peter Abelard—

'Let our hearts suffer for Thy passion, Lord,
That sheer compassion may Thy mercy win.'

*   *   *   *

In an attempt to capture something of the atmosphere, the unique atmosphere of Gregynog at Festival time, here are a few extracts from written impressions of one of the guests present at the 1936 Festival:

'One special charm of the Festival was that of being able to hear music and poetry in country surroundings, instead of in some bleak hall or city! To dream over the opal-like Monets, or look out on to lawns, trees and sky was to realise a little of the Greek ideal of the inseparability of Art and Nature . . . Another particular joy, that of being allowed to creep in to the rehearsals at any moment of the day, ranked high. There was the thrill of hearing fine artists at work in the surroundings of peace and leisure. The air all day was literally "full of sweet sounds that give delight and hurt not" . . . Other impressions gather—the lovely far-away voice in which Elsie Suddaby sang, the amazing range of the small choir, Mary Jarred's glorious tones . . . Keith Faulkner's glorious zest—to some one of the purest pleasures because one of the most rare, must have been that of hearing verse read as one has only dreamed of its being read . . .

One's mind went back again and again to the Greeks—their delight in music, poetry, painting, all art, wedded to good fellowship, laughter, beautiful surroundings, games; these were all abundant at Gregynog and we gratefully revelled in them.'

*   *   *   *

There was to be one memorable 'Matthew Passion' on Maundy Thursday, 1939 before the European War broke out, and all activity became subjugated to the war effort. Ironically, the actual final concert by the Gregynog Choir and Sir Walford took place away from their beloved music room. This was a choral recital given at the Village Hall, Llandinam in December 1940; in aid of the Lord Mayor's National Air-Raid Distress Fund. Sir Walford conducted patriotic songs and seasonal carols, closing with the music of his beloved Bach, 'Jesu, joy of man's desiring', and the piece that was Walford for so many people, 'Wachet Auf'. Four months later he died, and the memorial service at Gregynog signified the end of an era in that lovely house.

There were to be no more conferences, and no more concerts until 1954. Miss Gwendoline Davies, C.H., having died in 1951, Margaret Davies attempted to bring music back to the house with the help of Professor Ian Parrott, a successor to Walford Davies as Gregynog Professor of Music at Aberystwyth. Much respect was paid to the past, there was 'Music-Making by Students and Staff of U.C.W.' in 1954 (recalling the early Retreat of 1921), the newly formed Guild for the Promotion of Welsh Music held a conference in 1955 (recalling the arduous deliberations of the Council of Music), and in 1956 the Festivals were re-started. Much credit is due to Professor Parrott for faithfully maintaining the traditions of the house, with the inclusion of favourite music from pre-war days, such as Elgar's 'Music Makers' in 1956 and Holst's 'O Spiritual Pilgrim' in 1958.

Although each Festival consisted of but the one concert, it was richly endowed with well chosen music, performed by the revived house choir, the U.C.W. Chamber Orchestra, two old friends of Gregynog, Elsie Suddaby and Charles Clements, and many new friends drawn from the ranks of Welsh solo singers.

The curtain finally fell in 1962, with Margaret Davies's gracious gift of the house to the University of Wales. The last service, on Sunday, 29 April, drew its inspiration from the many lovely services of the past, including Walford's introit 'God be in my head', Holst's 'O Spiritual Pilgrim', Psalm 23, the passage 'Where shall Wisdom be found?' and, to close, the hymn which so perfectly expressed the faith and ideals of Gregynog,

> These things shall be: a loftier race
> Than e'er the world hath known shall rise
> With flame of freedom in their souls,
> And light of knowledge in their eyes.

CHAPTER SEVEN

THE DAVIES ART COLLECTION

ROLLO CHARLES

THE story of the formation of the Davies Collection has been told by Mr. John Ingamells, and he has described the French works, which are its most important component, both collectively and singly. His book remains the chief public salute to the two public benefactresses.

Briefly, Miss Gwendoline and Miss Margaret Davies formed their joint art collection between 1908 and 1924. In England they bought mainly through, and on the guidance of, Hugh Blaker, who was the brother of their companion and former governess. He was at different times a painter, poet, curator and dealer, and at all times a great enthusiast for latter-day French art. Their chief agent in Paris was the dealer Emile Bernheim. Miss Gwendoline stopped buying pictures in 1924, at the time when the sisters moved into Gregynog. Miss Margaret bought nothing between 1924 and 1934, when she began again, and continued for the rest of her life, acting partly on her own judgement and partly on that of other advisers.

Today almost all of the pictures and sculptures that they bought belong to the National Museum of Wales. But the sisters' purpose of collecting for the public perhaps matured slowly. It was never declared. The Misses Davies inherited great wealth. They were philanthropists, and keenly loyal to Wales. They were also art-lovers. The point is worth dwelling on. Were they, when they bought their unfashionable impressionist pictures, aware of being far-sighted? Certainly they bought with complete conviction; bought pictures for the walls of their own home in Wales and of their flat in London; pictures to live with and to love.

This is a salient feature of the collection. Miss Margaret's numerous purchases towards the end of her life bespeak a keen pleasure in patronage and the act of collecting. She knew well enough by then that public taste had caught up, and that the core of the joint collection was very notable indeed. Her later purchases were not nearly so significant as the early ones; but it was the pleasure that the pictures gave her which mattered.

They were art-lovers; not connoisseurs. They assembled no great library of monographs and periodicals, no archive of relevant photographs. Vetting was left to the vets, and their selection was made by eye.

The collection has never yet been described as a whole. In their lifetimes the sisters made several substantial gifts to the National Museum of Wales, of works by Rodin, Burne-Jones and Augustus John. Their joint collecting was, it seems, a matter of joint taste, but when Miss Gwendoline died in 1951 those works which she had herself paid for passed to the National Museum, so the joint collection was temporarily divided. Meanwhile, Miss Margaret was still buying. After her sister's death she sold some pictures by artists well represented in the collection (Turner, Daumier, Monet, Cézanne, Vlaminck) in order to buy others not represented (Sisley, Bonnard, Utrillo, Marquet, Kokoschka). She decided, at some time, that her pictures by contemporary and less famous artists should be treated as a loan collection for touring. All her pictures passed to the National Museum when she in her turn died, in 1963. She stipulated, however, that certain pictures should remain at Gregynog. She also left two sculptures by Rodin to the University of Wales, and gave a collection of etchings by Dürer, Rembrandt, Whistler, and others, to the National Library of Wales.

Some of the Misses Davies's gifts in life—large bronzes by Rodin, for example—never entered under their roof at all, coming straight to Cardiff when purchased. Other works were placed on protracted loan at the Tate Gallery and elsewhere. The works now belonging to the National Museum of Wales are scattered in the different picture-galleries and the Print Room there, or are away on tour. It has thus never been possible to see the entire Davies Collection in one place.

The works permanently at Cardiff can for convenience be grouped in four categories: Old Masters; British eighteenth/nineteenth-century works; French nineteenth-century works; and modern British and French works. Consideration of the parts may give an impression of the whole.

It should be prefaced, however, by the mention of an acquisition of a different and uncharacteristic sort. One day in 1920 the sisters paid a visit to the Leicester Galleries, the source of many picture purchases. They came away possessing a number of fine pieces of early Chinese, Greek and Islamic pottery. This seems to have been an impulsive purchase.

Pottery was never a major interest, though they furnished Gregynog with handsome late Persian wares as decoration. Miss Margaret gave many of these early pots to Cardiff after her sister's death.

The Old Masters are a small group, of less than a dozen. Most of them were bought from Blaker. Blaker's eye, so sound when it was a matter of recommending Impressionist painters, was less reliable when he was buying and selling Old Master paintings. True, he for a time owned a version of the Mona Lisa which some scholars think may be by Leonardo himself, and the original portrait at that; but of the Old Master pictures which he sold to the Davies sisters, not all can sustain the weighty names which he attached to them. Two, a 'Teniers' and a 'Velazquez', are of no standing whatsoever. A *Portrait of a Lady,* once published as a Hals, is now attributed to him with some doubt. A small panel of *The Deposition,* once attributed to Van Dyck, is now attributed to Abraham van Diepenbeeck. There are three pictures which were labelled El Greco: two are somewhat remote from the master, but the third, a half-length version of the *El Espolio* in Toledo Cathedral, is of better quality. It is very uneven in execution, and much damaged and restored, but at any rate not the unworthiest of the many studio versions of that picture which exist, and the central faces might perhaps have been painted by El Greco himself. Another excellent picture is the circular *Madonna and Child with St. John* from the studio of Botticelli. This is a tender work, almost identical in detail and at least as fine in quality as a similar picture in the National Gallery. Perhaps it is not by the master himself, but it is very near.

The sceptical probing of attributions is a healthy and necessary activity, particularly with pictures which have become public property. The addition of the words 'Studio of' to names on frames does not alter the merit of the pictures themselves. With the continual increase of specialist critical knowledge, the work and achievement of the great masters is continually clarified and, one hopes, better understood. Botticelli's assistant and El Greco's assistant are worthy surrogates here for the great men themselves, to testify to the spiritual crises of their times. The same can be said of the (presumed) Diepenbeeck, though the aspect of the mighty Van Dyck here reflected was itself a reflection of the even mightier Rubens. The so-called Teniers is, it seems, an imitation; but Dutch genre painting is well represented by Benjamin Cuyp's picture of *The Blind leading the*

Blind, and Dutch protestantism by a small *Adoration of the Kings* by Rembrandt's pupil Van den Eeckhout, signed and dated 1665.

The acquisitions of the three El Grecos is of some historical interest. This artist's wide popularity today is hardly two generations old, and gained ground (in this country) more or less in step with Cézanne's, who purveyed a similarly astringent emotional flavour. It seems quite natural that if Miss Gwendoline was impressed by the one artist she should have been impressed by the other. It is also interesting to recognise in El Greco the source of certain mannerisms of pose in Augustus John's work.

The Old Masters are a haphazard collection, Florentine, Spanish, Dutch and Flemish. The collection of English eighteenth / nineteenth century works is rather more comprehensive, but besides its splendours it too has certain idiosyncracies.

The sisters were collecting at the time when Lord Duveen was making his fortune by exporting resounding English portraits to the United States of America, at resounding prices. The names of Reynolds, Gainsborough and Lawrence must have conjured up visions of grandiose and over-expensive full-lengths, and it is certain that the Misses Davies would want no such pictures on their secluded walls. They never bought Reynolds at all. The few portraits they did buy, by Romney and Raeburn and Lawrence, are no bigger than half-lengths, and unpretentious pictures of women and girls. They were only interested in Gainsborough as a landscapist. Moreover, a whole era of British painting is almost entirely missing from their collection—the generation of artists who were born between 1800 and 1830 and whose prime years spanned the middle of the century: the artists of their grandfather's day. He was the founder of the family fortune, and was painted by Ford Madox Brown; but the grand-daughters never owned that picture, and their collection included no Pre-Raphaelite work, no High Victorian painting. Those years are abundantly represented by French artists. British painting only appears again with the Grosvenor Gallery artists, Burne-Jones (1833–98) and Whistler (1834–1903).

Their earliest British picture was also their best, and Welsh at that: one of Wilson's loveliest landscapes, *Penn Ponds, Richmond Park.* Recent cleaning has revealed this as a particularly majestic and luminous work. Its early history is unknown, but it presumably dates from the period of the artist's full maturity, in the 1760s. It too epitomises a moment of sensibility, a moment of particular balance between classical form, valid because profoundly believed in, and individual response to nature. The Davieses owned another Wilson, and two little landscapes in the 'picturesque' style of Gainsborough, but these are of minor appeal compared to *Penn Ponds*.

The pictures they bought to represent the great landscape painters of the next generation are frankly uneven. There are a number of works in the manner of Constable, which critical opinion will not accept. There are also seven oils by Turner, over which critical opinion remains divided. These last are all in the style of the 1830s and '40s, that distinctive style of misty radiance. Many have tried to imitate it while lacking the inimitable draughtsmanship on which it was based. Some of the Davies pictures have pedigrees leading back to the family of Turner's last housekeeper; but the falsification of his pictures began as soon as the artist died (as it did with Constable and Wilson). Some of the Davies oils seem to be pastiches. Some may be beginnings finished by other hands. One or two may be authentic but not particularly good Turners.

But if the Turner oils are disappointing, the Davies's eight remaining watercolours (some were sold) are of very high quality. These range from a detailed picture of *Rye* made about 1824 for the series of engravings of the *Southern Coast*, to later studies of Alpine scenery which verge on the abstract. Moreover, these watercolours have escaped the constant over-exposure which has been the ruination of so many.

Watercolours as such were not collected however. There are an early Blake, generally entitled *Christ trampling down Satan* , and several Welsh views by the prolific Welshman Moses Griffith; but no Girtin, nor Cotman, nor De Wint. Cox is represented by three oil-paintings. There are also two paintings by Barker of Bath: a big landscape *The Cattle Fair,* and a self portrait. It seems likely that it was their associations with Wales that attracted the sisters to these last two artists.

The splendid quality of the Davies French pictures needs no stressing. In a short essay it might be enough merely to mention the highlights. No serious student of the artists will neglect the groups of works in the collection by Daumier, Millet, Cézanne, Monet, Renoir and Rodin. These artists are represented at their greatest strength, and it is tempting to leave discussion there. Yet Manet and Pissarro are represented hardly less importantly, and the single pictures by Morisot, Van Gogh, and the later artists Derain and Bonnard, are typical and memorably beautiful. Again, the dimensions of the collection can be mapped by listing the main absentees: Courbet; Degas (as a painter) and Toulouse-Lautrec; and Seurat. One might offer a guess that Courbet was too red-blooded a radical for the sisters' liking; that they had no wish to contemplate women in bathtubs, or the Parisian *demi-monde*; and that Seurat was too austerely intellectual. Ingamells stresses the quietist character of their pictures, rightly, even though they do include a landscape by Manet painted in Paris during the harsh winter of the siege of 1870, and an agitated painting by Van Gogh made within a few days of his suicide. Extremes, either of social realism or of artistic theory, were avoided.

These artists are among the immortals, and the pictures by them in the Davies Collection are now part of the international art-currency. The Collection nevertheless gains enormously in interest, indeed in meaning, from the additional presence of works by their less famous contemporaries: and it is in this general area of nineteenth/twentieth century painting, English and French, that its bulk resides. There is a certain period flavour about it. Who, today, collecting the Impressionists, would also buy Meissonier, Matthieu Maris or Mancini? Who, today, is much concerned about Bargue or Van Maestenbrock? Some artists have long since sunk into a sort of art-historical compost: but Mancini was a friend of Sargent; Meissonier was Manet's company-commander during the siege of Paris; Mauve, Lhermitte and Monticelli were admired by Van Gogh. The Collection also illustrates that general Anglo-French *entente* which encompassed Whistler; Burne-Jones, Puvis de Chavannes and Augustus John; Degas and Sickert; and the English impressionists like Clausen and Steer. The relationships between great artists and lesser need to be seen, for the proper appraisal of both kinds. Fertilisation across the Channel was fruitful and not entirely one-way. And there are still other themes to be explored in the Collection, and contrasts offered: the gentle landscapes of Corot, Diaz and Boudin with the violent ones of Friesz and Vlaminck; the same building painted, at about the same time, by Monet and Sickert; the expressive use of light by Daumier, Carrière, and Pryde; and so on.

A collection in which so rich a texture can be woven with the work of major and minor artists together, has far greater liveliness than any mere assemblage of masterpieces.

Interest in later British painting had two main roots. The tradition most strongly followed was the middle-of-the-road realism centred on the Slade School. Steer and Sickert are well represented, and so are the Camden Town artists, and Matthew Smith, the Nash brothers, and Hitchens. There was no 'modernism' as such, e.g., by Bomberg or Ben Nicholson, and no academic naturalism. Wyndham Lewis and Spencer are represented, but by portrait-drawings only.

There is also a numerous and varied Welsh element, encompassing such odd bed-fellows as Brangwyn, Ceri Richards, and Mr. Kyffin Williams. Augustus John is particularly strongly represented, mainly through works bought by Miss Gwendoline Davies from early exhibitions held in the Chenil Galleries. These include an arrogant self-portrait of about 1920, and the equally fine portrait of W. H. Davies. The work of Gwen John was perhaps not available to Miss Gwendoline during her buying days, but it is surprising that Miss Margaret never acquired any work by an artist whose temperament might have appeared so sympathetic to her own: nor did she buy anything by Mr. David Jones, although he was commissioned to illustrate *Ecclesiastes* for the Gregynog Press. But the roll-call of their artists still provides a remarkably impressive conspectus of Welsh and English twentieth century painting.

CHAPTER EIGHT

THE GREGYNOG PRESS

DOROTHY A. HARROP

ONE might well speculate as to how and why a private press of undisputed distinction came to be established in the heart of rural Wales, a country which can lay singularly little claim to participation in the production of fine books. To attempt to answer these questions it is necessary to explain something of the circumstances, interests and aspirations of the two sisters whose wealth and influence called it into being.

The Gregynog estate, consisting of the house, some 750 acres of land and a handful of farms, was acquired in 1914 jointly by David Davies, later the first Baron Davies of Llandinam, and his sisters, Gwendoline Elizabeth and Margaret Sydney. The house was let between 1914 and 1919, and in July, 1920 the estate was formally conveyed to Miss Gwen and Miss Daisy, as the sisters were known. They had been educated largely at private and finishing schools, as befitted ladies of their class at that time: neither went to university. Both were musically gifted, and both were intensely interested in the arts, as evidenced by their early support of struggling artists and by the acquisition of the collection of paintings, described elsewhere. Their interest extended to craftwork of all kinds.

The sisters had inherited considerable wealth, and after the First World War were seeking ways of deploying it and of spending their days in meaningful pursuit. To lend their names and donate sums of money to a succession of causes, though they did that too, was not sufficient. Gwen Davies in particular was deeply conscious of a debt to humanity, since their wealth had accrued mainly due to the sweat of workers in South Wales, employed in the family coal mines and other commercial enterprises. What more fitting way than to use Gregynog Hall as a rehabilitation and training centre for some of those whose lives had been torn asunder by the war? Here, in this peaceful setting, they planned to train men and women in furniture making, pottery, weaving and printing. Peter Waals, the celebrated Gloucestershire cabinet maker who had worked for Ernest Gimson, was summoned early on to carry out a feasibility study on furniture making. His report was not encouraging. Though the estate sawmill was in good working order, he considered the standard of local craftsmanship rough and well below that to which he was accustomed in the Cotswold villages.

For help and counsel in these matters the sisters turned to Dr. Thomas Jones, then Deputy Secretary to the Cabinet, whose acquaintance they had made in 1910 when he had assisted their brother as Secretary to the King Edward VII Welsh National Memorial Association, a national campaign against tuberculosis. T.J., as he was widely known, was an influential figure in Wales and in the larger arena beyond. His interests were legion and his circle of acquaintance wide. He was to become an ally in all their undertakings, acting as friend, confidant, adviser and link with the world outside. No vital decision was ever made without recourse to his advice, and it is doubtful whether, without his constant support and encouragement, any of their enterprises would have progressed beyond the blueprint stage. Constantly at their beck and call, no task was too menial for him, even to the extent of forgoing his holiday in 1920 to oversee matters at Gregynog where he secured the services of an architect to carry out alterations, interviewed house and garden staff and acted as general consultant. His influence on the sisters is incalculable. Of particular interest here is his influence in the foundation of the Gregynog Press. It has been said, with some justification, that though the Davieses may have footed the bill, it was really T.J.'s press. Certainly without him it could not have existed. From his circle of acquaintance in the fields of literature and bookmaking were to be drawn all the authors, editors and translators for the Gregynog publications and all the contacts made to secure the services of the craftsmen who were to contribute to the success of the Press.

Printing featured early on in the sisters' plans, for in 1920 T.J. was commissioned to try to obtain the equipment, imprint and good will of the Shakespeare Head Press,[1] a venture which proved abortive. Attention was turned to the appointment of a controller of the proposed craft

---

[1] The Shakespeare Head Press, founded 1904 at Stratford-upon-Avon by A. H. Bullen who died in 1920.

centre. Through the good offices of Hugh Blaker,[2] who had acted as their adviser when acquiring their collection of paintings, a meeting was arranged between the sisters and Robert Ashwin Maynard, an artist in whom they had become interested before the war when he had exhibited with the London Group at the Goupil Gallery. He had later become a successful painter of theatrical scenery, prior to being commissioned in The Royal Fusiliers. Maynard, disillusioned by war, was currently employed as a salesman for a Shrewsbury manufacturer of cattle medicines. Though he at first protested that he knew nothing about crafts, he became so caught up in the web of infectious enthusiasm that he agreed to give up his post in January 1921 to spend time in London, at the Davieses' expense, learning something of the techniques involved.

Meanwhile the reconstruction of the outbuildings at Gregynog to provide accommodation for the various crafts moved so slowly that the sisters grew discouraged, and talk of some of the crafts died away. By June 1922, however, a print shop and composing room were ready. The idea of printing at Gregynog was firmly rooted, never to be dislodged. New ideas for activities were now promulgated which included exhibitions of paintings, summer schools for art teachers and lantern lectures for schoolchildren. Though Maynard did later run one summer school and experimented with pottery made from Gregynog clay, mention of these activities gradually faded. The vision, as originally conceived, had receded somewhat.

Maynard's knowledge of printing, typography and wood-engraving was limited to the little he had managed to acquire in London. He now set out to improve that knowledge by practice. On 20 December, he recorded in his notebook the pulling of the first printed proofs on an Albion hand press made specially by Stephenson Blake Ltd., and on 27 December 120 copies of a Christmas card were printed. This, the first of many Gregynog Christmas cards, was a modest but laudable attempt, printed in 14 point Kennerley type on Japanese vellum, inserted in a blue-grey Ingres paper cover. The insert comprised a four-line verse and simple wood-engraving depicting the Hall, signed by Maynard. It is of typographic interest to note that Maynard had not yet learned to omit the full point at the end of a line printed in capital letters, a slip rectified in the next piece of printing.

---

[2] Hugh Blaker, 1873–1936, artist, connoisseur and art critic. One-time curator of the Holburne of Menstrie Art Museum, Bath.

21 February 1923 saw the installation of a Victoria powered platen press made by Messrs. Huddon. This machine was to do yeoman service, for on it were printed most of the Gregynog books and all the items of a more ephemeral nature. A month prior to this, John Hugh Jones, a youth from Anglesey, had joined the staff as an assistant. He was to remain at the Press until its close and was to prove a great asset. For some years he was the only member of the staff who was capable of proof reading a Welsh text. In March John Mason, the son of J. H. Mason[3] who had been working as manager of the Eyre and Spottiswoode bindery at Eton, was appointed bookbinder and general assistant.

In May 2,000 copies were printed of an account of the origin of the *Annual Good-Will Message of the Children of Wales,* together with the text of the first broadcast message, issued on behalf of the Welsh Council of the League of Nations Union. Here Maynard experimented with the use of paragraph marks and initials printed in red, and his name appears in the colophon. He was working hard at improving his wood-engraving technique, and in June appeared a broadside bearing J. Ceiriog Hughes's poem, *Rhyddid,* surmounted by a wood-engraved landscape, printed in black and blue. The following month two programmes for concerts held at Gregynog during the conference of The National Council of Music were printed. These bear the first known press device—a wood-engraved GG[4] monogram set on a fir clad mound and, beneath, the caption LEVAVI OCULOS.[5]

The printing of ephemeral items was to remain a continuing activity. From 1921 fairly frequent conferences were held at Gregynog, and for each one after 1930 the Press printed a form of religious service and often a conference programme. These, together with publication prospectuses, programmes for concerts and the festivals of music and poetry, held 1933–8, and the annual Christmas card, formed the bulk of the printed ephemera. Some 240 items have so far been traced but must lie outside the scope of this brief survey. Two items, the *Annual Good-Will Message of the Children of Wales* and the certificate for the annual Urdd Gobaith Cymru National Eisteddfod, were the only ones regularly printed for

[3] J. H. Mason, 1875–1951. Assisted T. J. Cobden-Sanderson at the Doves Press, 1900–9. Assisted Count Harry Kessler to establish the Cranach Presse at Weimar and resumed work there, 1928–9. Co-founder of *The Imprint.*
[4] Gwasg Gregynog.
[5] Twenty-eight different devices in all were used by the Press.

outside bodies. All the ephemera are competently printed but, apart from a few exceptions, are of no more than passing aesthetic interest.

The first book, *The Poems of George Herbert,* selected by H. Walford Davies, was begun on 3 July, completed on 9 November, and published on 7 December, in time for the Christmas market. Three hundred copies were printed in 12 point Kennerley type on Grosvenor hand-made paper. It has a wood-engraved frontispiece and initial letters by Maynard and was bound by John Mason in paste-marbled paper, made at the Press, with a cloth spine. Due to printing on dry paper, the inking and impression appear somewhat uneven, and the initials are inferior to Maynard's later work. Nevertheless, this chaste little volume remains a remarkable achievement. Its appearance did not pass unnoticed in the world of fine books, doubtless due to the efforts of T.J. Praise was instantly forthcoming from several notable bibliophiles, and Bernard Newdigate later reviewed it favourably in the *London Mercury* for 11 November 1925.

In February 1924 Idris Jones,[6] a local boy, was appointed general assistant and Horace Walter Bray, an old friend and fellow student of Maynard, artist. Maynard, by this time, had settled down happily, and his skill as a typographer and wood-engraver was gaining maturity. Having cut a number of blocks, he now felt confident enough to instruct Bray in the technique. Towards the end of his life Maynard was to recall these early days at Gregynog as the happiest of his career.

The Davieses had never intended living at the Hall, but in April 1924, family differences caused them to move out of the family home at Llandinam and into Gregynog. The rest of their lives they were to spend between Gregynog and their London flat which was at 3 Buckingham Gate. About this time a small but powerful board of directors was formed. Its membership comprised T.J., as Chairman, Gwen and Daisy Davies and Ernest Rhys, editor of Dent's Everyman series, as literary adviser. Publishing policy naturally formed a large part of their early discussions. Their aims at this time were threefold—to publish Welsh works in translation in as accurate and fine format as possible, to reproduce the best work contributed to English literature by Welsh writers and to produce fine editions of texts in the Welsh language. These aims were adhered to strictly until 1930. Though the Davieses had no intention of making a profit out of their publications, they did express a hope that

---

[6] Idris Jones was later printer to the National Library of Wales until his retirement in 1974.

the Press would one day be self-supporting. Alas, like every other private press, it never achieved this happy state. Books in Welsh were subsidised from the sisters' personal funds to sell at a cost below that of their production, yet most of them sold slowly, for Welsh people had little money to spend on fine books and scant experience in the appreciation of them.

Maynard was naturally ambitious for the Press and, following the example of several major private presses, advocated the design of a special type face for its exclusive use. After discussion, Edward Johnston[7] was approached. His terse reply, 'I am rather loath to design a new type until I see better use made of what we have—or a real need for it', must have pricked the bubble of the board, for the matter did not crop up again for another decade.

Poems by Henry Vaughan, selected by Ernest Rhys, was published in December 1924, a year after the first book, to which it is similar in all respects: Kennerley type, Grosvenor Chater paper and woodcut initials in red were all used again. Maynard and Bray worked jointly on the thirteen illustrations and the initials. Unfortunately, some of the latter appear somewhat too wide for the page setting. The book is bound in grey Ingres paper covered boards, blocked in blue with a monogram of the poet's initials and the Swan of Usk, designed by Maynard, and dark blue cloth spine. In May 1925, the Press issued its first book in Welsh, *Caneuon Ceiriog: Detholiad,* edited by J. Lloyd Jones. Here the Kennerley type sits well on the page, and the initials begin to show improvement. Thirty-one simple wood-engravings by Maynard and Bray form head- and tail-pieces. The covering material is white linen, perhaps an unfortunate choice, used with a cloth spine.

As Maynard's expertise as a book designer increased he hankered to use other type faces. A Monotype caster was therefore installed which, by purchasing the appropriate die cases, would allow him a wide choice. After the first four books, Kennerley was abandoned for good.

That summer John Mason, who had become frustrated over the non-appearance of a promised house, resigned. The gap was filled for two months by Sydney Cockerell[8] who did some forwarding in the bindery

[7] Edward Johnston, 1872–1944, calligrapher and teacher of lettering. Author of *Writing, Illuminating and Lettering,* 1906.
[8] Sydney Cockerell, born 1906. Bookbinder and son of Douglas Cockerell.

and experimented with paper marbling. In November George Fisher was appointed binder. Fisher was a gifted craftsman of long experience who had formerly worked in the Rivière London bindery. His contribution to the success of the Press is incalculable. He caused separate accommodation to be provided for the bindery (binding had previously been carried out in part of the press room), trained and directed assistants recruited from local schools, improved the standard of the ordinary cased bindings and was personally responsible for the production of the superb full leather bindings which were later given to between fifteen and thirty copies of each edition.

R. O. Jones of Newtown was appointed compositor to the Press in the Spring of 1926. With increased staff and problems of accommodation alleviated by the construction of a studio for Maynard and Bray, work could proceed at a faster pace. For the first time two books were published in the same year. *Detholiad o Ganiadau gan T. Gwynn Jones* was ready in January. It is an unremarkable little book, printed in Kennerley type on smooth, creamy Dutch paper, illustrated with nine simple head- and tail-pieces by Maynard and Bray and bound in peacock blue buckram. Sales were encouraging, for it was out of print by the end of the year. *Chosen Essays by Edward Thomas,* selected by Ernest Rhys, was published in November. Fifty copies were printed on handmade paper watermarked GG and the remainder on Van Gelder. The type chosen was 14 point Garamond, a face re-cut by Monotype in 1922 and as yet not much used in Britain. The choice was a happy one, for it looks well on the larger page format used here. A frontispiece portrait and twenty-three other illustrations by Maynard and Bray display a lighter touch with the graver than hitherto.

Mrs. Dora Herbert Jones, a friend who had helped Gwen Davies with the running of her wartime canteen for the troops in France, had been travelling for some time from Aberystwyth on one day each week to assist with proof reading and much needed secretarial work. In April 1927 she took up a permanent appointment as Secretary to the Press and private secretary to the sisters. Well known as a singer and collector of folk-songs, she and Gwen Davies had many interests and tastes in common. Miss Gwen came to rely on her heavily in matters connected with cultural activities at Gregynog. She assisted in arranging the religious services held during conferences and the programmes of the festivals of music and poetry, and it was after her advent that the Gregynog choir was formed. Her position was not an enviable one—a friend, a ready help in times of need and yet an employee whose main function was to act as secretary, public relations officer and saleswoman to the Press. The dual role cannot have been an easy one for an intelligent woman of cultivated tastes and with a mind of her own who cared passionately about the maintenance of high standards and who came to put loyalty to the Press almost before anything else.

Her appointment was followed within three weeks by that of Herbert John Hodgson as printer. Hodgson, a Londoner, had already achieved distinction as a printer with W. H. Smith & Sons and later as assistant to Manning Pike in printing the first limited edition of T. E. Lawrence's *Seven Pillars of Wisdom* which was supervised by the author himself. Hodgson came to Gregynog on the recommendation of C. H. St. John Hornby[9] and until 1936 was responsible for the superlatively high quality of printing at the Press which was the envy of connoisseurs of fine printing everywhere.

Selected Poems of Edward Thomas, edited by Edward Garnett, was published in August, and all copies were subscribed for within a week. It is a beautifully designed work, printed in Garamond type on Japanese vellum, and displays Maynard's growing mastery of the classical title-page. It is undecorated except for an interesting title-page device in blue and large wood-engraved shadow initials in red. The text pages have pale blue marginal rulings.

During 1927 Maynard first showed signs of the restlessness that was to torment him until his resignation in 1930. Interference in Press personnel matters on the part of the estate manager rendered him uneasy. He had striven to inculcate a spirit of enthusiasm and adventure among his staff but now found that he had no control over matters concerning their social welfare, a state of affairs which he bitterly resented. Increasingly he suffered from a sense of isolation from other artists, for Gregynog offered scant artistic stimulus apart from its beauty and solitude and he and Bray were also beginning to feel the strain of being entirely responsible for all the illustration and decoration.

[9] C. H. St. John Hornby, 1867–1946. Director of W. H. Smith & Son Ltd. Owner of The Ashendene Press, 1895–1935.

That summer the Press undertook to prepare an edition of Sir John Morris Jones's Welsh translation from the Persian of Omar Khayyam's *Rubaiyat* which had previously appeared in his *Caniadau*. T.J. had conceived the idea of publishing it in time for the National Eisteddfod held in August at Holyhead, but plans went awry. A straight reprint was out of the question as Sir John had found errors in the version already published. Furthermore, Maynard's idea of embellishing it with simple Persian type ornaments did not satisfy the translator. He hankered for a properly illustrated edition and was frankly shocked by the proposed haste. There ensued a protracted discussion by correspondence between translator and controller concerning the text setting and illustrations which taxed Maynard's patience sorely and which delayed publication for a further eighteen months.[10]

Experiments were made at this time in printing on vellum, but the results were disappointing due to the inherent instability of this material which stretches in printing and thus increases the problem of obtaining correct register for subsequent printings on the same sheet. This not only affected printing in two colours but the use of illustration also, as the wood-engravings were always printed separately from the text at Gregynog. Eventually the attempts were abandoned: the splendid vellum editions of other private presses found no rival here. Two copies of *Llyfr y Pregethwr* and a simple Christmas card for 1928 are the survivors of these experiments.

The Life of St. David, edited by Ernest Rhys, was published in November 1927. This slim quarto, the bravest Gregynog experiment in decoration so far, was the first book to be printed on damped hand-made paper. Odd though it may seem, Maynard had only recently learned of this almost universal practice. The unfamiliar method caused some problems in printing, and the presswork is not always as even as it might be. Nevertheless, it is a delightful book. The text has paragraph marks in red ink drawn with a quill by Horace Bray. The Poliphilus type, printed in black, red and blue, is apt and dignified, but the most outstanding features are the twenty-five illustrations by Maynard and Bray, delicately hand coloured by girls working in the bindery. The title-page, composed of wood-engraved titling in blue, an illustration of the saint redrawn

---

[10] The correspondence is reproduced in 'The Gregynog Omar Khayyam', by David Jenkins in *The National Library of Wales Journal*, xvii, 51–87.

from a brass in Hereford cathedral and a small blue cross beneath the imprint, is one of the best to emanate from the Press. The binding of the ordinary edition is in plain limp vellum.

Publication day was shared by *Llyfr y Pregethwr: the Book of Ecclesiastes*. The wood-engraved crucifixion frontispiece and title-page are by David Jones. These lack harmony: the frontispiece is much too black and heavy for the facing page. Poliphilus type was an injudicious choice, for ideally it requires closer setting than the Welsh text permits, and the cruciform paragraph marks appear over large. It is a competent if somewhat dull book.

The year 1928 was to be the heaviest publishing year, apart from 1933, in the history of the Press. In April appeared *An Account of the Convincement, Exercises, Services and Travels of that Ancient Servant of the Lord, Richard Davies,* a book plain and sober as its title, printed in Baskerville on Batchelor paper and unillustrated, the only spot of colour being the red title-page device. As a piece of straight printing it is well nigh flawless, but it is a dull book for all that, and the drab navy blue buckram binding is about as interesting as an office account book.

There was a significant change in format for the next book, *The Autobiography of Lord Herbert of Cherbury,* a handsome folio, printed in Poliphilus and Blado types, which was published in May. The admirable title-page is decorated with a hand coloured shield bearing the arms of the noble lord, and on the recto following, appears a beautiful wood-engraving of the reclining figure of Lord Herbert by Bray, after the painting by Isaac Oliver. There are eight other fine engravings by Bray, full of intricate detail, which are quite unlike any of his previous work. The fine lines of these are superbly printed by Hodgson on the rough hand-made paper. On several pages a large wood-engraved initial opens the text in a manner similar to that found in old illuminated manuscripts, and the dignity of Poliphilus is shown to perfection. This book is one of the outstanding achievements of the Press and was one of the few Gregynog books to call forth reviews which commented at length on its physical attributes.[11]

The second book to be printed on Japanese vellum, *Selected Poems of W. H. Davies,* edited by Edward Garnett, was published in November.

---

[11] The *Observer,* 10 June 1928, review by J. L. Garvin. The *Manchester Guardian,* 25 June 1928, review signed H. B. C. (H. B. Charlton, Shakespearean scholar).

It is unillustrated except for a frontispiece portrait of the poet by Maynard, after the portrait by Augustus John, nicely complemented by a graceful title-page which bears a new large press device in yellow and black. Following the pattern of the earlier volume of Thomas poems, the margins are ruled in feint red which helps somewhat to redress the balance of the verse settings ranged on the left.

Thomas Love Peacock's *The Misfortunes of Elphin,* published later the same month, includes no colour. The twenty-three head- and tail-pieces by Bray are cut in a simple woodcut style, depicting squarish figures. There is much demure drollery in these spirited little engravings which adds greatly to the book's charm.

Penillion Omar Khayyam, on which Maynard had laboured for so long, was finally published in December. It is sympathetically set in Caslon type and has an attractive title-page printed in blue and black. Maynard's ten wood-engravings, which had occasioned much of the protracted dialogue between translator and controller, turned out to be something of a triumph after all. Despite the extreme attention to detail given to this book by the translator, he overlooked an initial to mark the opening of quatrain XLI when proof reading which was not discovered until after publication. At his instigation the sections containing the offending leaf were reprinted for the copies later bound in levant morocco. Alas, Sir John did not live to see the correction in print, for he died the following April.

The year 1928 ended on a tragic note, for on 21 December an event occurred which shattered the little community at Gregynog. T.J.'s youngest child, a boy of twelve, was killed by a car near his Hampstead home. A clever, quick-witted child with a wisdom beyond his years, Elphin was the treasure of his father's heart. To Gwen Davies later that day T.J. wrote, 'The lively life is ended—brutally, stupidly, and the ability and the fun and the old fashioned sense finished . . . I feel as though I had no feeling.' The following March the Press printed for private circulation, *Elphin Lloyd Jones: a Memoir,* a pleasing little booklet of twenty-four pages, which contains memories by the parents, a reproduction of a school essay and three wood-engravings by Maynard.

The only book published in 1929, the *Psalmau Dafydd gan William Morgan,* edited by Ifor Williams, was the most ambitious of the Welsh publications. It is printed in red, blue and black in Poliphilus type with foliated openings and decorated initials designed and engraved by Bray. The verse settings are beautiful, but the title-page and special openings may appear over ornate to some eyes. Bray also designed the paper for the binding which was printed at the Press.

To the utter stupefaction of all concerned, Maynard and Bray announced their joint resignation in February 1930, though they later agreed to stay on, pending the appointment of a suitable controller. Before their departure in the early autumn three more books were printed. *Christina Rossetti: Poems,* published in April, is a fairly ordinary book, printed on Japanese vellum with initials and a wood-engraved portrait by Maynard. *Elia and The Last Essays of Elia,* by Charles Lamb, a beautiful two volume work, illustrated with a series of wood-engravings, after contemporary prints, by Bray, was completed in March, although not published until eleven months later. The illustrations are its chief feature. Of great charm and delicacy, they lend to the book a delightful period flavour. *The Stealing of the Mare,* by Anne and Wilfrid Scawen Blunt, was completed on 1 July and published in November. Printed in Garamond on heavy Japanese vellum, this has an attractive title-page in black, blue and gold, followed by a superb wood-engraved double opening with gold and colour applied by hand. The text is embellished with decorated initials, also hand coloured. The decoration was the work of Maynard who also designed the foliated patterned paper, printed at Gregynog, which is featured in the binding. This is, without doubt, one of the most beautiful of the Gregynog books.

Maynard returned to supervise the printing of the last book after his departure. This was the two volumed *Plays of Euripides,* translated by Gilbert Murray.[12] Beautifully set and printed in Bembo and Fairbank Italic each folio volume has sixteen wood-engravings drawn from fifth century Greek vases by Maynard and cut by Bray. For this book the Press used James Morton's recently devised anti-fade Sundour bookbinding cloth.

Maynard and Bray were responsible for producing eighteen of the published books, most of them illustrated or decorated. Maynard had

---

[12] Two years earlier the Press had sought permission to reprint the text of this free of charge from Stanley Unwin, Chairman of Allen & Unwin Ltd. who owned the copyright. Their request brought forth a characteristic reply: 'The press may be a labour of love, but the productions are not given away, and I am not clear why the owners of the press should not pay a royalty . . . as other publishers have to do.' The contretemps was settled by the Board agreeing to pay a royalty of 15% of the published price.

THE GREGYNOG PRESS, TITLE-PAGE OF *Psalmau Dafydd*

succeeded admirably in establishing the reputation of the Press which was now widely respected for the standard of its productions. Though this reputation was later upheld, and many fine books were still to come, rarely was the typographical standard equalled in later years. Maynard's achievement appears all the more remarkable in that he had never received any formal training in book production.

Shortly after George Fisher's appointment in 1925 it had been decided to bind a small number of copies of each edition in full leather. Fisher himself was responsible for the covering and finishing of these bindings which rapidly became much sought after by collectors. After the first,[13] seventeen special bindings were designed either by Maynard or Bray, in conjunction with Fisher. All are in levant morocco and are fairly plain. Some have decoration tooled in gilt or gilt and blind, laid out in traditional geometric form. They are simple and sometimes rather austere bindings in which the beauty of the leather and Fisher's skill in forwarding are seen to advantage.[14]

When Maynard and Bray had left to found the Raven Press in Harrow Weald, Hugh Blaker again came to the rescue of the Press Board in recommending Blair Hughes-Stanton for the vacant post of controller. Stanton, then twenty-eight years old, was an artist of Welsh extraction, the son of Sir Herbert Hughes-Stanton, R.A. Both he and his wife, professionally known as Gertrude Hermes, who was also a sculptor, were already well known as wood-engravers. Stanton was offered the post of controller, but wishing to be free of administration, suggested a friend, William McCance, a painter and sculptor, for the position. McCance was married to Agnes Miller Parker, another wood-engraver of repute. Thus it came about in May that McCance was appointed controller and Stanton artist to the Press. Neither had any knowledge of printing, and each was sent to a printing firm for a short period of intensive training, McCance to Charles Knight's works and Stanton to the Baynard Press.

For their first piece of printing, an order of service used in November, Stanton cut a new large press device depicting a snail shell.[15] which was used on several items of ephemera but never on a book. Their first book,

---

[13] The first special binding was by John Mason.

[14] For a more detailed account of the special bindings the reader is referred to the author's 'George Fisher and the Gregynog Press' in *The Book Collector,* Winter, 1970.

[15] This design was based on one supposed origin of the name—*cregynnog* = abounding in shells.

an illustrated edition of W. H. Davies's *The Lovers' Song Book,* was not approved by the Press Board who considered the typography poor and the illustrations unsuitable, and publication was postponed. As *The Plays of Euripides* was currently in production, their first published book, Milton's *Comus,* 1931, was printed on the hand press by Idris Jones. This, printed on Japanese vellum, has an illustrated title-page and six superb costume engravings by Stanton. He also designed the special binding in biscuit coloured levant which is decorated with broad per-pendicular panels of fine blind lines, contrasted with broad lines in gilt.

The illustrated books of this period are outstanding, those illustrated by Stanton and Agnes Miller Parker being of particular note. Though two books illustrated by Gertrude Hermes were planned, they were never published,[16] and it reflects little to the credit of the Press Board that they let slip the opportunity of using the talent of this extremely gifted artist.

Stanton's highly individual style caused comment among Gregynog collectors, and, perhaps not surprisingly, his apparent preoccupation with the unclothed or scantily dressed human figure was frowned upon in some quarters. The fine flowing lines and meticulous detail of his wood-engravings display a technical mastery which has not been surpassed in the entire history of the medium. These illustrations are the work of a highly charged imagination, many of them marked by a kind of savage dexterity. His best work apart from *Comus* is seen in *Four Poems by John Milton,* 1933, illustrated with eleven engravings, *The Revelation of St. John the Divine,* 1932, a folio printed in Bembo with Perpetua titling in black and Tyrian red, with a magnificent engraved title-page and forty-one other engravings of incomparable skill and virtuosity and *The Lamentations of Jeremiah,* 1934, printed in Baskerville italic in black and blue. This has a dramatic engraved title-page, five full-page engraved chapter openings and fourteen other engravings, many of which depict restless and often contorted figures, nude or clothed in diaphanous drapes. *Lamentations* provides a good example of successful continuous text setting in italic. These books are truly a visual feast.

For Samuel Butler's *Erewhon,* 1933, Stanton cut twenty-nine wood-engravings in quite a different style, singularly apt and of great charm.

---

[16] Gilbert White's *Natural History of Selborne* and another version of W. H. Davies's *The Lovers' Song Book.*

Sadly, the title-page of this book was a typographical disaster, as contemporary critics were swift to point out. All of these books are printed on Japanese vellum, the smooth surface of which shows up the delicate lines of the engravings to perfection. A specially dense black ink was also imported from Germany to heighten the effect. There is a considerable contrast, between these illustrations and those in *Caniadau gan W. J. Gruffydd*, 1932, where the four pictorial engravings are adversely affected by being printed on a rough stone-tinted hand-made paper.

Agnes Miller Parker provided the wood-engravings for Caxton's *The Fables of Esope*, 1932, and *Twenty-One Welsh Gypsy Folk-Tales*, collected by John Sampson, 1933. An almost equally fine engraver, her style and technique are quite different from Stanton's. Her animals have a living, breathing quality of almost three-dimensional aspect which display a liquidity of movement astonishing in so static a medium. Unfortunately, these beautiful illustrations suffer a little from being placed none too sympathetically on the page and by being closely crowded by type.

Undoubtedly the work of these two fine artists was greatly enhanced by Hodgson's incomparable printing skill. It would be well nigh impossible to find wood-engravings more sympathetically printed anywhere.

Engravings by McCance are found in Vansittart's *The Singing Caravan*, 1932, which has a fine frontispiece portrait printed in black and brown, and in O. M. Edwards's *Clych Atgof*, 1933, where the chapter openings are decorated with small engravings in brown, many of which are quite pleasing if somewhat mechanical but which are marred by the overprinting in black of the initial letters and by being too closely crowded by type.

Typographically the books do not compare with Maynard's work, for McCance never seemed to come to grips with type. His settings are idiosyncratic and marred by an undue use of double rule underlinings of titles and chapter headings and by a lack of space between illustrations and type areas. His engraved initials appear over large so that the pages tend to have a fragmented look, and his use of brown ink combined with black becomes boringly repetitive. Stanton and McCance were perhaps an ill-assorted pair, for their work, unlike that of Maynard and Bray, was widely different. It must be conceded that Stanton's elongated figures were not easy to match with type on the conventional format of the printed page. To make a harmonious whole required typographic skill of a very high order.

With the advent of Stanton and McCance the design of the special bindings changed dramatically, and Fisher was afforded better opportunity to display his skill as a finisher. Of Stanton's bindings, one much admired is that on *Erewhon,* but this is largely due to the virtuosity of the tooling. Artistically it is not to be compared with his designs for *The Revelation of St. John the Divine* and *The Lamentations of Jeremiah.* The former, bound in cream levant, displays on each cover a crushed panel, the larger one on the upper cover bearing symbolic designs, including a black cross onlaid and gilt lettering with fine shading, which is contrasted with a brick-red onlay, lettered and shaded in blind. The title appears on the upper cover and the imprint on the lower. The covers of *Lamentations* are identical. The black levant has an onlaid disc of dark blue, shaded with gilt and blind lines, from which hangs an avenging sword, over onlaid squares of diminishing size, outlined in gilt, their bases linked by a diminishing arrangement of lines, while a fine gilt line connects them diagonally to the upper part of the design.

McCance's two binding designs are both arresting. On *The Fables of Esope* the main feature is the ingenious arrangement of the word ESOPE on the front cover, onlaid in reddish-brown on cream levant. The binding of *The Singing Caravan,* covered in orange-brown oasis, has an unusual eastern style fore-edge flap, and the decoration comprises a complex arrangement of lines, enhanced by small black onlays, extending across both covers.

Somewhat to the relief of the Press Board, the contracts of McCance and Stanton were terminated by mutual consent in September 1933. The period of their tenure had not been an easy one. The two families had never settled happily at Gregynog, and the volatile temperaments of controller and artist had led to deterioration in staff relations within the Press. Partly for this reason their talents never seem to have been fully appreciated by the Board. Never again was there to be a resident controller or artist at Gregynog.

The Davieses felt that, for the time being at least, they had had a surfeit of artists. Having been somewhat disappointed in McCance as a typographer, they hoped to find a controller with proved typographic skill. John Johnson, printer to the Oxford University Press, recommended Loyd Haberly, a young American, who, after a brief career at Harvard University, had come as a Rhodes scholar to Oxford where he had

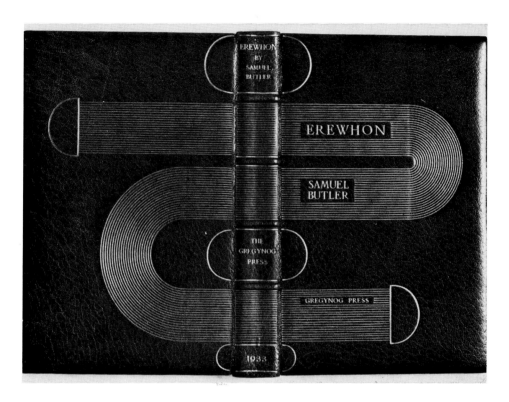

THE GREGYNOG PRESS, ONE OF THE FINE BINDINGS

taken a law degree at Trinity College. A man of artistic leanings, he was currently running his own small private press, The Seven Acres Press, at Long Crendon in Buckinghamshire. Johnson wrote of him to T.J., '[He] is that blend of dreamer and practical man which it is so difficult to find in life. It is a blend which you more often meet, if I may say so, in your race than mine.' Having invited Haberly to Gregynog, the Davieses were anxious to engage him. Haberly, however, had too many interests of his own to want to immure himself in such remote surroundings, but eventually agreed to act as controller on a part-time basis.

Meanwhile, that autumn, the Press busied itself printing two books. These were W. H. Davies's *The Lovers' Song Book* which was published at last in December, in a simple, unillustrated edition and T.J.'s *A Theme With Variations,* a book of reminiscences, which was printed for private circulation.

Haberly officially joined the staff in January 1934, but it soon became apparent that he preferred to work on designing the books away from the Press and had small desire to participate in the mechanics of running it. Inevitably this was to cause problems and delays in publication. *Don Quixote: an Introductory Essay in Psychology,* by Salvador de Madariaga, a well printed but otherwise undistinguished book, was published the following September. The next book, Haberly's own *Anne Boleyn and Other Poems,* appeared in November. This has hanging titles in red and initial letters, drawn for line block, by Graily Hewitt, printed in red and green, a colour combination for which Haberly obviously had a particular liking, for it was used again in Henry Thomas's translation of *The Star of Seville,* attributed to Lope de Vega, 1935, to the pages of which the raw red and green lend a spotty effect.

Robert Bridges's *Eros and Psyche* is undoubtedly the most interesting though not the most successful book of this period. For this Haberly commissioned Graily Hewitt to redraw a type used by Johann Neumeister of Mainz in his edition of Dante's *Divina Commedia,* printed at Foligno in 1472. This, which later became known as Gregynog type, was cut for the Press by Monotype. The design is too eccentric for continuous reading, and certainly it is too heavy for the illustrations which accompany it in *Eros and Psyche.* Its only other appearance at Gregynog was in the 1935 Christmas card, for the words of an old Welsh carol, where it was accompanied by a music type, specially designed for the Press by Haberly and Graily Hewitt. Gregynog type was adversely criticised by several typographical pundits of the day, with the result that it was abandoned.[17] The illustrations in *Eros and Psyche* were redrawn by Dorothy Hawksley from the Burne-Jones designs intended for William Morris's *Cupid and Psyche,* a book which was never published. Unfortunately, when printed, these were but pale imitations of the original designs.[18]

The most outstanding publication designed by Haberly is Xenophon's *Cyrupaedia,* 1936, which H. W. Garrod, writing in The *Observer* for 13 December 1936, described as 'a book of lordly sumptuosity'. A handsome folio, magnificently printed in Poliphilus in red and black, its text is well set, with ample margins and pleasing foliated initials designed by Haberly. Its weakest feature is the title-page which appears as a crowded conglomeration of capital letters.

Though never described as such, Haberly's last book, Fortescue's *The Story of the Red Deer,* 1936, is really a children's book. Cloister type here made its only appearance at Gregynog. The book represents the only example where colour printing was used at the Press for illustrations. The simple pictorial illustrations, drawn for line block by Dorothy Burroughes, are printed in four poster inks, specially mixed by Herbert Hodgson.

On 5 December 1935, Stefan Mrozewski, a Polish artist and wood-engraver, visited Gregynog to supervise the printing of 350 copies of Helen Waddell's poem, *New York City,* to which he had contributed a startling wood-engraved frontispiece. One hundred of these, signed and numbered, were used for private circulation, while the remainder were distributed as Christmas cards.

Due to Haberly's infrequent visits to supervise work through the Press, relations between him and the Press Board had become somewhat strained. Also he expressed a desire to be free to follow other pursuits, with the result that his contract was terminated abruptly in December 1935. His *Eros and Psyche,* an interesting and expensive experiment, had misfired, and, of the books printed under his direction, only the *Cyrupaedia* can justly lay claim to distinction. Books which he later produced in the United States display considerable talent. Had he come to the Press later

---

[17] Later the types were taken to the United States by Haberly where he used them to better effect.
[18] Further information concerning the history of these illustrations is given in J. R. Dunlap's *The Book that Never Was,* Oriole Press, 1971.

in life perhaps the books would have been different. Yet perhaps not: at Gregynog he had been expected to fit into a mould predetermined by the nature of the Press and circumscribed by a somewhat inflexible Press Board, but Haberly's wayward whimsicality was not a thing to be grasped and pinioned.

Of the special bindings of this period three were designed by George Fisher, that of *Cyrupaedia* being the most ingeniously devised and that of *The Story of the Red Deer* artistically the best. Stanton provided the simple symbolic design of onlaid stars and gilt lines which appears on *The Star of Seville,* and Haberly was responsible for the unimaginative geometric design on *Anne Boleyn.* John Ewart Bowen[19] was apprenticed to Fisher in 1935, and thereafter, the cased cloth and paper bindings of the ordinary editions were replaced by bindings in full leather, in order to provide suitable training for him.

The fine book trade had been in the doldrums for the last few years, due to the slump, and the Press had been steadily losing money, so that at the end of 1935 its future seemed uncertain. Herbert Hodgson resigned in February 1936, and Dora Herbert Jones's duties were restricted to those of private secretary. The old order was changing, and the running of the Press was left temporarily in the hands of John Hugh Jones.

After much searching, a new controller was eventually found in James Wardrop of the Victoria and Albert Museum. Neither typographer nor artist, Wardrop was an authority on Italian manuscript hands and a calligrapher of minor distinction who had taught evening classes in book production for the London County Council. By October the printing of Fulke Greville's *Caelica* was completed under his direction, Idris Jones having succeeded Hodgson as printer. Typographically it is a relatively uninteresting book, as perhaps befits such dull poems. Stanton was again commissioned to design the special binding which is decorated with vellum stars onlaid on slate blue levant.

Wardrop's chief contribution to the Press, and undoubtedly one of its crowning achievements, was Joinville's *The History of St. Louis,* translated from the French by Joan Evans, published in December 1937. The setting, in 16 point Poliphilus with marginal rubrics in Blado, enhanced with initials and special openings, printed alternately in red and blue, designed by Alfred Fairbank and cut by John Beedham, is magnificent.

[19] John Ewart Bowen is currently binder to The National Library of Wales.

There are seventeen coats of arms, printed from wood-engravings by Reynolds Stone and hand coloured, which are exceedingly rich but which might have benefited by being placed elsewhere on the page, and two maps drawn by Berthold Wolpe. The book was deservedly an immediate success.

The last five books in design and printing bear all the marks of assured competence but lack the distinction of some former works. Hartzenbusch's *The Lovers of Teruel*, 1938, is undeniably the least inspiring. Antonio de Guevara's *The Praise and Happinesse of the Countrie-Life*, 1938, the smallest Gregynog book, displays a sympathetic use of Bell type on smooth hand-made paper and has some charming head- and tail-pieces by Reynolds Stone. Its crowded title-page is less successful. This was the only book issued in a dust wrapper. *Shaw Gives Himself Away*, 1939, is printed on pale green tinted paper and has a frontispiece portrait engraved by John Farleigh. By the time the last two books were ready for printing, Idris Jones was serving in the armed forces, and Hodgson, who had been working for Maynard at the Raven Press, returned to Gregynog in 1940 to print them. The bilingual *Gweledigaethau y Bardd Cwsc: Visions of the Sleeping Bard,* by Ellis Wynne, has a frontispiece engraved by Stanton which harmonises well with the rather anaemic title-page. Lascelles Abercrombie's *Lyrics and Unfinished Poems* is of interest mainly for the use of Van Krimpen's Romulus type, specially imported from Holland, a type hardly seen at that time in Britain. The page format seems over large for the short verse lines which causes the otherwise elegant type to appear insignificant.

Two other items worthy of mention designed by Wardrop are Milton's ode *On the Morning of Christ's Nativity* with a frontispiece engraved by Alison Mackenzie, an eight page pamphlet, distributed as one of the 1937 Christmas cards, and *John Davies,* a memoir of the Secretary of the South Wales District of the Workers' Educational Association, issued for private circulation the following summer.

Of the special bindings of the seven published books produced under Wardrop, those of *Caelica* and *The Lovers of Teruel* were designed by Stanton though they are not to be compared with his earlier binding designs. Wardrop himself designed that of *The History of St. Louis,* decorated with a fleur-de-lys semis, and the last four are by George Fisher. A Paul Nash design for the special binding of *Shaw Gives Himself*

Away was rejected by the Press Board, but he did furnish that of the ordinary binding. The semi-abstract design, based on the author's initials, onlaid in orange on dark green oasis, is refreshingly different from the other designs.

By 1939 war seemed inevitable. The Davieses moved their valuables from London to Gregynog; the annual festivals of music and poetry were abandoned, and talk of books grew less. In October Wardrop was drafted into the Ministry of Supply. In his three-and-a-half years as controller of the Press, only five books had so far been published, and in December it was suggested, none too tactfully, that he should resign, which he duly did, leaving two books planned but not yet printed. Wardrop's books are marked by good taste, a classic simplicity and a seemingly innate desire not to step out of place. On his going, T.J. observed ruefully to Gwen Davies, 'I regret that so rarely are we able to part with any Press employee in a quite unclouded atmosphere.' It is a sad indictment of relations between the Board and staff at Gregynog that his words rang all too true.

One by one the staff drifted away into war service, and Gwen Davies found cause to remonstrate with T.J. concerning his ready acceptance of closure. 'It won't be possible to open the Press ever again once we close down . . . don't give up our dreams like this without a struggle.' Alas, there was no possibility of continuing. The last book, printed in June, was published in August 1940. Gregynog was shortly to become a Red Cross convalescent hospital for wounded servicemen. George Fisher stayed on alone until 1945, finishing the special bindings which had always been in arrears.

In February 1946, the Press Board met to discuss the possibility of re-opening but decided that this was not feasible. Hope destroyed, Gwen Davies wrote touchingly to T.J. a letter of appreciation. ' . . . the [Great] war had knocked my life and health to pieces, and it all had to be re-built . . . and you were the builder and restorer. We planned and worked together. I do want to thank you from the bottom of my heart for all you have given me and done for me . . . All I have been able to do during the last thirty years has been almost entirely your doing.' She died, aged sixty-nine, on 3 July 1951 in the Radcliffe Infirmary, Oxford. Her sister who, though joint owner of the Press, had never really had the same interest in it, survived her by twelve years. T.J. himself died on 15 October 1955.

The Press, over a period of eighteen years, enjoyed a deservedly distinguished reputation in the world of fine books. It maintained throughout a standard of excellence virtually unrivalled elsewhere. This was due, in no small measure, to the standards set early on by Maynard, to the quality of materials used and to the amount of time and care lavished on the preparation of the books, such as no other press could afford. Editions were small, ranging between 150 and 500 copies. Of the forty-two published books, thirty-one were printed on hand-made paper and the remainder on Japanese vellum. Thirteen type faces were used in all, Baskerville, Bembo, Poliphilus and Perpetua being the most favoured.

As in the case of most private presses, Gregynog's contribution to literature was small: few of the books published were original texts. Nearly all of them lay in the fields of Welsh and English literature, sixteen of them being books of poetry. Eight books are in the Welsh language and eleven more have some affinity with Wales, yet the Welsh element is in a somewhat diluted form. Though assistants in the Press were recruited locally, none of the guiding hands on the production side was Welsh. The Davieses were of Welsh blood but did not speak the language, and their cultural affinities lay largely beyond the confines of the Principality. Neither of the sisters had any practical knowledge of printing: in that respect Gregynog must be virtually unique in the history of the private press movement. They took no part in the day to day running of the Press, Gwen Davies visiting it but rarely, Daisy Davies hardly ever.

ACKNOWLEDGMENTS

THE author would like to record her gratitude to the following who have given help and advice: Baroness White of Rhymney and Tristan Jones, Esq. for permission to consult the papers of their father, the late Dr. Thomas Jones, C.H.; the late Miss Jessie Adams; John E. Bowen, Esq.; Sydney Cockerell, Esq.; the Hon. Islwyn Davies; Mrs. Gwen Edwards; Dr. Joan Evans; the late George Fisher, Esq.; Dr. Loyd Haberly; Miss Gertrude Hermes; Herbert J. Hodgson, Esq.; Blair Hughes Stanton, Esq.; Dr. Glyn Tegai Hughes; Idris Jones, Esq.; Idwal Jones, Esq.; and the staff of the National Library of Wales. The complete collection of Gregynog books and extensive collection of ephemera belonging to the late Mrs. Dora Herbert Jones were ever at my disposal until her death. My debt to her is incalculable.

BIBLIOGRAPHY

BLAKER, HUGH, 'The Drawings and Engravings of R. A. Maynard', *Studio*, xcix, 443 (February 1930), 95–102.

BOWEN, JOHN EWART, 'Memories of Gregynog', *The Manchester Review*, viii (Spring 1959), 264–8.

CAVE, RODERICK, *The Private Press*, London, Faber, 1971, 376 pp.

CHILD, HAROLD, 'The Complete Book-Builder: a Survey of the Gregynog Press', *Studio*, xcix, 445 (April 1930), 277–82.

DAVIES, GWENLLIAN M., 'The Gregynog Press: a Talk to the Manchester Society of Book Collectors, 16 October 1958' *The Manchester Review*, viii (Spring 1959), 257–63.

DAVIES, GWENLLIAN M., 'Loyd Haberly: a note on his printing, plus a checklist of the books from 1925 to 1960 compiled by Loyd Haberly', *The Manchester Review*, Autumn 1962, 311–20.

DAVIES, J. MICHAEL, *The Private Press at Gregynog*, Leicester College of Art, 1959, 20pp.

DUNLAP, JOSEPH R., *The Book that Never Was*, New York, Oriole Press, 1971, vi, 86 pp.

FLETCHER, IFAN KYRLE, 'Two Books from the Gregynog Press', *The Welsh Outlook*, xv, 1 (January 1928), 15–16.

FLOWER, DESMOND, 'A Survey of Modern Binding', *Signature* 9 (July 1938), 19–32.

FRANKLIN, COLIN, *The Private Presses*, London, Studio Vista, 1969, 240 pp.

GAMBLE, WILLIAM, 'The Gregynog Press', *Penrose's Annual*, xxxi (1929), 129–31.

HABERLY, LOYD, 'Loyd Haberly: Poet and Printer', *The Printing Art*, i, 3 (Autumn 1973), 2–13.

HARROP, DOROTHY A., 'George Fisher and the Gregynog Press', *The Book Collector*, xix, 4 (Winter 1970), 465–77.

HARROP, DOROTHY A., 'The Gregynog Press', *Encyclopaedia of Library and Information Science*, New York, Dekker, x (1973), 196–202.

HERBERT JONES, DORA, 'The Gregynog Press', *Rural Industries*, xi (Summer 1928), 3–4.

HERBERT JONES, DORA, 'Sir John Morris Jones', *The Welsh Outlook*, xvi, 5 (May 1929), 137–8.

HUTCHINS, MICHAEL, *Printing at Gregynog. Aspects of a Great Private Press/Argraffu yng Ngregynog. Agweddau ar Wasg Breifat Fawr*, transl. by David Jenkins, (Cardiff), Welsh Arts Council, 1976, 38 pp. Published on the occasion of the Council's Gregynog Press Exhibition.

JENKINS, DAVID, '*Caniadau* Gregynog' (i.e. the T. Gwynn Jones volume), *Y Traethodydd*, cxxvi, 538 (January 1971), 28–32.

JENKINS, DAVID, 'The Gregynog *Omar Khayyam*', *The National Library of Wales Journal*, xvii, 1 (Summer 1971), 51–87.

JENKINS, DAVID, 'Gwasg Gregynog', *Llais Llyfrau*, vi (Winter 1966), 1–5.

JONES, JOHN HUGH, 'The Gregynog Press', *Life and Letters Today*, March 1940, 226–35.

JONES, JOHN HUGH, 'The Gregynog Press', *The Montgomeryshire Society Year Book*, 1935–36, 42–47.

JONES, THOMAS, 'Art in National Life: Ubiquity of the Press in Wales: Makers of the Gregynog Books', The *Western Mail*, 21 December 1925.

JONES, THOMAS, *The Gregynog Press: a Paper Read to the Double Crown Club on 7 April 1954*, London, Oxford University Press, 1954, 40 pp. (This contains a bibliography of the Press).

JONES, THOMAS, 'The Gregynog Press', *The Welsh Outlook*, xv, 8 (August 1928), 249–50.

LEWIS, JOHN, 'The Wood-Engravings of Blair Hughes-Stanton', *Image*, 6 (Spring 1951), 26–44.

MAYNARD, ROBERT ASHWIN, 'The Gregynog Press with a Private Type Foundry,' *The Monotype Recorder,* xxviii, 232 (September–October 1929), 17–19.

NEWDIGATE, BERNARD, *The Art of the Book,* London, Studio, 1938, 104 pp. (=Special Autumn Number of *The Studio*).

RANSOM, WILL, *Private Presses and their Books,* New York, Bowker, 1929, 493 pp.

RANSOM, WILL, *Selective Check Lists of Press Books,* New York, Duschnes, 1945, 420 pp.

SYMONS, A. J. A., 'Modern English Bindings at The First Edition Club Reviewed', *The Book Collector's Quarterly,* 13 (January–March 1934), 81–6.

TOMKINSON, G. S., *A Select Bibliography of the Principal Modern Presses,* London, The First Edition Club, 1928, xxiv, 238 pp.

WILLIAMS, WILLIAM, *Private Presses with Special Reference to Wales,* London School of Printing, 1938, 12 pp.

CHAPTER NINE

THE PARK AND THE GARDENS

'B. S. O. FOX

THE gardens are in a wonderful setting, not only the immediate woodlands, but the whole surrounding countryside. The natural grouping of small wooded hills is a splendid background for any type of planting and is, of course, the same kind of country as that in which Powis Castle and Gardens stand. As a measure of the way in which plants can grow in this area, it is worth noting that in similar Montgomeryshire countryside grows a Douglas Fir that is the tallest tree known in the British Isles.

Apart from the splendid natural setting, there is evidence of landscape work involving considerable earth movement especially close to the mansion itself.

The earliest record of a garden design for Gregynog comes from a plan drawn up in 1774 for Arthur Blayney by the landscape designer William Emes (died 1803), who worked in the manner of Capability Brown, and whose hallmark was a serpentine series of lakes. Emes worked in a number of places in the late 1760s and 70s, which Blayney may have visited: Powis, Chirk, and Erddig (this last the home of Philip Yorke, Arthur Blayney's biographer). The Gregynog design, with its vast informal plantings and its series of pools and lakes, was typical of Emes. It is not known how many of the projected lakes were formed, but a number were later drained, and only one or two now survive. The observant eye can still see where some of them must have been. One almost expects to find a lake in the sunken garden in front of the house.[1]

So much for what might have been, all we can do now is to trace the course of later developments as we know them. The first information comes in 1913 when the whole estate was sold. The sale catalogue of

---

[1] A copy of the Emes plan is preserved in the Gregynog MSS. in the house. The editors wish to thank Dr. K. M. Goodway of the department of biology at the University of Keele for his help concerning the career of William Emes, and also to thank Mr. Austen Wilks of Saint David's University College, Lampeter, for references to him.

this date shows one or two photographs and descriptions of the more permanent garden features that were then present and also some of the short term plantings of interest.

From the 1913 information we can establish that all the large scale earth moving to form the terraces and the sunken garden close to the mansion had been completed some time. Also present were the paths of the woodland walk to the south-west which also include the flight of concrete steps and concrete bridge of the viaduct that crosses the drive leading to the rear of the mansion and over which one enters the woodland proper. The tree covered mound up which the concrete steps lead was surely intended for some special treatment as a feature before crossing the viaduct, but on this we can only speculate.

The walled garden of nearly an acre and the glasshouse unit were present and could be approached along the drive leading to the south-west and on which stand the garden cottages, or arrived at off the end of the woodland walk. Another feature noted in the catalogue was the terra-cotta fountains.

Regarding the plantings it is evident that many introduced conifers were well established, and some of these close to the mansion would appear from a photograph to be some forty feet high at that date. These included a variety of spruce and silver fir, but no species were actually named in the catalogue.

The unusual golden yew hedge on the bank bordering the sunken garden was well established in 1913. This bold planting can hardly fail to attract the attention of any visitor and cause him to speculate as to what had been originally intended. Firstly, this feature must have been deliberately and carefully planned, and the very large number of golden yew plants would have had to be specially grown for it from cuttings or grafted plants. Secondly, plants live by growing and any piece of topiary develops according to the treatment it receives. We now view it with its broad back and stubby legs, but it must have been quite slender in the first place. The 1913 catalogue shows a photograph of it still in quite slender form with the relatively larger spaces between the 'legs' planted with roses, and it must then have been a most colourful parterre garden.

In the sunken garden area below the yew hedge there were rose and flower parterres, but these would seem to have been short lived as were the string of flower beds along the bank above the yew hedge which were later replaced by the rock bank. The planners at this stage must have been intrigued by unusual hedges, for two short hedges of osmanthus survive at the approach to the bridge over the sunken garden, and in the sale catalogue there is mention of a sweet briar hedge of two hundred yards in length.

The final piece of information we have about this period is a mention of ' . . . magnificent Rhododendron plantations' and it is interesting to note that the variety 'Pink Pearl' had special note. Although this gaudy flowered form is now one of the most commonly grown it had then only recently been distributed by J. Waterer & Sons, having received an award by the Royal Horticultural Society in 1900.

Little is known of what happened in the garden between 1913 and the purchase of the property by the Misses Gwendoline and Margaret Davies. This period, of course, included a number of most austere years during the first world war when maintenance costs were doubtless cut to the absolute minimum.

Certainly the rose and flower parterres were grassed over and in this same period, or possibly in the years immediately following the war, cherry laurels and other suitable subjects were planted as cover for pheasants.

From the time that the Misses Davies came to Gregynog much more is known about the development of the grounds and certainly plant-wise this was the start of a whole series of new features and planting schemes. Again there are no plans and no written records so that we are indebted to Mr. George C. Austin, Head Gardener from 1930 till his retirement in 1969, for his recollections and remarks on the past.

It seems that of the two sisters it was Miss Gwendoline Davies who was most interested in the garden and it was she who initiated most of the planting schemes. In those days it really was a ladies garden for the Head Gardener was a Miss Clark and her assistant a Miss Durrant. Both these ladies worked in the garden for many years and the latter stayed on after the appointment of Mr. Austin. This petticoat rule must have had a profound effect on the gardeners in the bothy by the walled garden and one wonders how they regarded their lady colleagues and their employers 'Miss Gwen and Miss Daisy'.

At this time most of the construction work was carried out by con-
tractors, and one such development was the pool garden to be seen off
the south side of the main drive. A duck pond existed on the site, but
there was much work to do and this included the laying on of water,
also the erection of a boat house and a summer house.

Even today as one stands under a fine old oak looking across the pool
now overgrown by water-lilies and other aquatics, surrounded by the
more prolific forms of iris and although now completely dehumanised,
it is not difficult to picture it at the height of its development. Boats on
the water, people in the summer house, a path around the perimeter of
the pool with beds of primulas, astilbes and *Hosta ventricosa*. The grass
round the oak and on the approach to the pool was planted with narcissus
and *Anemone apennina*. The pool garden was designed and constructed
by Messrs. R. Wallace & Co. of Tunbridge Wells as was the rock bank
above the yew hedge by the mansion; the lady gardeners however had
much to do with the planting of the rock bank.

Mr. George Austin was appointed Head Gardener in September 1930
and this was the start of a period of intense gardening activity. Firstly,
the landscape architect, Mr. Avray Tipping, was called in to draw up a
plan for the dingle and this was the first of a series of natural woodland
type plantings that took place during the thirties. The dingle, now
overgrown, rises to the north of the old walled garden and must not be
confused with the dell that lies north-east of the mansion and was
developed later.

It is hard to imagine what the dingle looked like when in its prime,
though one or two photographs survive, for at the outbreak of the
1939–45 war it was decided amongst other economies that this feature
would have to be abandoned. From that time nothing whatever in the
way of maintenance was carried out in the dingle and it is interesting
to see which plants survived and in some cases even thrived. The survivors were in the main species of waterside and woodland plants, but
there were also a few early hybrids and garden varieties, all vigorous,
but of graceful form; how many present day varieties of garden plants
could stand this test?

Amongst the waterside plants rise the massive leaves of *Gunnera
manicata*, also the more lowly *Rodgersia pinnata* and *R. aesculifolia*. Needless
to say the bamboos also held their ground well as did the large form of

filipendula and early tall garden forms of astilbe such as the dark red variety 'J. Ophorst'. Many subjects failed in the struggle with indigenous plants and amongst these were the plantings of lilies. The shrubs on the higher slopes did not fare so well either and only the rose and philadelphus peep out beneath the advancing canopy of woodland trees.

At the upper end of the dingle there is evidence of a dam and small pool. There must have been a lot of earth and rock to move for this because it is known that a railway was built to help with the work.

In about 1932 following the planting of the dingle, the 'bank' was planted. The bank in question being the south facing slope covering the area roughly between the woodland walk and the drive out to the gardener's cottage and walled garden. Most of the planting is on the north-east end of it that borders the drive where it turns to go beneath the viaduct and the rear of the mansion.

A very wide range of interesting shrubs and small trees were planted and these included a number of flowering cherries. A footpath runs the length of the bank and various bulbs and cyclamen were grouped at strategic points along it though there is little surviving evidence of this. The shrubs and small trees are somewhat stifled due to overcrowding and some are stunted because of thick grass growing right up to them. This would seem to be a suitable point at which to mention what was the one horticultural great failing of the Misses Davies. They were most reluctant to thin out plants or to prune them in any way, so that once planned and planted the various subjects were left to develop as they would. This is an interesting point for, when planning with living material, things do not always turn out as the planner expects, small changes have to be made and it is necessary to know what the ultimate aim is.

In 1933 the idea of the dell was conceived. The dell seems to have been gradually developed over a period of time and although this is one feature that has been maintained over the years, it was in its heyday much more extensive than it is now.

Astilbes, gunneras, erythroniums, trilliums and peltiphyllums were planted and are still cultivated. Trilliums take a considerable time to establish but these have a strong hold now and are seeding themselves about. Another plant that has thrived is *Peltiphyllum peltatum* whose pink flowers rise from the bare rhizomes in spring and are followed by saucer shaped leaves which after a shower of rain soon fill the boots of the unwary jaywalker. At the lower end of the dell was a bridge and by this a collection of Asiatic primulas. Plantings of this nature however require constant attention and this feature would seem to have been discontinued during the war.

During the pre-war period there was a gradual build-up of staff. When Mr. Austin came in 1930 there were sixteen gardeners employed, including the lady gardeners who remained for many years, and by 1939 this number had risen to twenty-three. There was a small permanent staff in the dell and this was under the supervision of Mr. Arthur Hughes of Newtown.

'Miss Gwen' read many gardening books and took particular note of the works of A. T. Johnson who, of course, gardened under similar conditions in North Wales, and was an extremely useful source of information regarding the selection of plant species for various situations.

Mr. George Austin must have played an important role in the design of the garden as well as directing the work in his capacity as Head Gardener. To support this there is written on the flyleaf of a book by Avray Tipping 'To G. C. Austin, in sincere appreciation of the way he has designed and planted the dell at Gregynog from Gwendoline E. Davies, Easter 1933.'

The planting in the dell was added to for a year or so and then work continued on the opposite side of the drive where a woodland garden was developed. Little evidence remains of this due to subsequent heavy tree growth; however, there are three fine specimens of *Rhododendron auriculatum* whose large gloriously scented flowers make a splendid show in late summer.

Immediately before the war, between 1937 and 1939, the garden was at its peak of cultivation; the staff though large had to deal with many labour intensive features. There was a large herbaceous border that backed on to the rear drive and could be viewed from the windows of the mansion. This particular feature survived for many years, but there were many others that could not be maintained after the war. Old photographs show large beds of perennial plants and one dated 1938 is of an expanse of lupins, possibly at the north-east end of the bank.

Sometime around 1935 a unique hybrid plant arose by the lake side and was spotted by Mr. Austin. Although not widely planted, it is of considerable merit as a plant for the water side, and is worth mentioning here if only that it bears the name Gregynog. Unfortunately, it belongs to a group of plants whose nomenclature is somewhat involved but we would be correct here in calling it *Ligularia* 'Gregynog Gold'. In 1943 a detailed description of this plant appeared in the *Journal of the Royal Horticultural Society* (Vol. 68, p. 171) where Mr. A. T. Johnson wrote of it as a hybrid senecio.

The present day sees the garden in much more simple form, though the scene has changed due to trees reaching maturity and these are rather crowded in many places. Within the garden, tree growth has been variable. This is to be expected where isolated specimens are concerned. However, growth would also seem to have been affected by a change in water table. As in all gardens and woodlands the design materials are living matter and subject to constant change. No doubt the Misses Davies would have liked a more mature background for their colourful display of plants in high degree of cultivation. Today the cost of such efforts would be prohibitive but we must also ask ourselves if at this mature stage such displays would even be desirable.

In February 1972, Dame Sylvia Crowe, the landscape architect, produced a landscape report on the grounds and gardens,[2] in which she pointed out the need for a greater distinction between the woodland and garden areas, the need for simplification of certain features especially in the vicinity of the house itself, and also that more advantage should be taken of views of the surrounding country. She emphasised the need for maintaining the predominantly broadleaf character of the landscape, particularly upon the hilltops. It was suggested that more paths should be opened up, leading to selected views, and that there should be variation in the treatment of woodland areas so as to produce different types of woodland habitat. A number of these proposals have been put into effect. The University has also benefited from the advice and work on the management of the woodlands at Gregynog from the department of Forestry at the University College of North Wales, Bangor. It can be seen thus that although the park and the gardens are a work of art, within a framework centuries old, they are like a human society made of living material, and they are always changing, always developing.

---

[2] Gregynog MSS. Sylvia Crowe, D.B.E., P.P.I.L.A., 'Landscape Report on the Grounds and Gardens of Gregynog', February 1972.

CHAPTER TEN

THE BEQUEST TO THE UNIVERSITY

THOMAS PARRY

THOSE of us who were privileged to know Miss Margaret Davies and to have enjoyed her company and her hospitality at Gregynog realised that she had been very much exercised about the fate of Gregynog and its grounds after her own day. The house had been her home for many years, and there was gathered into it a noble collection of artistic treasures which were fit accompaniments to the musical activities and the fine printing for which the place was noted. The invaluable contents of the house could of course be safeguarded, but in an age when ancestral homes were ceasing to be the property of their owners and occupiers, and were sometimes being put to strange uses, it was natural that Miss Davies should wish to perpetuate and bequeath to others something of the cultural delight which she herself had experienced at Gregynog.

She had suggested in conversation, in her own shy way, that the University College of Wales, Aberystwyth, might wish to be associated with Gregynog in some way or other. From the very foundation of the College members of her family had shown a deep interest in its welfare and progress, and had been its prime benefactors. It would have been appropriate and gratifying for the College to be able to show its appreciation of the generosity of the Llandinam family by playing a part in meeting the wishes of the last representative of the third generation, and helping to preserve at Gregynog some of the standards and ideals which she and her sister, Miss Gwendoline Davies, had fostered there.

Further discussion, however, between Miss Davies and her advisers led her to believe that the most suitable body to approach was the University of Wales—a wise decision obviously. It was rumoured that Miss Davies was contemplating handing over Gregynog to the University —an act of generosity which, however amazing, was quite comprehensible to those of us who knew her and her family traditions. This was corroborated when the University Council, at its meeting on 20 November

1958, received a letter from Mr. E. C. Powell, Miss Davies's secretary, saying that she was prepared to hand over Gregynog, together with about 750 acres of land and a sum of money as an endowment, to the University, provided that an acceptable plan for its future use could be worked out.

All the Council could do then was to thank Miss Davies most warmly for the offer. The magnitude of the bequest and its novelty made it inevitable that very serious thought should be given to the responsibilities, as well as the possibilities, involved. It was felt that fairly firm proposals with regard to the use to be made of the house and the land should emerge before the offer could be formally accepted. Gregynog was centrally situated and reasonably accessible from all the Colleges, but whether the staff and students of the various institutions would feel disposed to make use of any facilities made available, there was at the time no means of judging.

As a first step the Council appointed the Pro-Chancellor and the Heads of the constituent institutions as a committee to consider the possibilities. This committee visited Gregynog and had talks with Miss Davies and her advisers. On 25 July 1959 the Secretary of the Council, Dr. Elwyn Davies, met Miss Davies's advisers in order to discuss certain financial matters. It was learnt that Miss Davies would provide £10,000 per annum towards the maintenance of Gregynog, with the possibility of an additional sum of up to £5,000. It was now up to the Council to formulate a general scheme for the use of Gregynog, and a special meeting was held on 28 August. To quote from the Secretary's letter to Miss Davies:

'The Council proposes that the primary use of the Hall shall be as a centre for the cultivation and enjoyment of the fine arts . . . The Hall will serve as a centre for the appreciation of the visual arts, for the practice and enjoyment of music, and for training in and exercise of dramatic art . . . It is proposed also that the Hall shall serve as a focus for joint work by selected students drawn from all the Colleges under the direction of a distinguished scholar; and as a centre for conferences, study groups and summer schools . . . The University would wish to be free to make the Hall available for use for the above purposes by other universities and other bodies . . . and to use it as a centre for meetings of its own administrative and academic bodies, and to entertain their visitors and guests whom it wished to receive into its fellowship.'

These proposals were acceptable to Miss Davies.

In all the discussions up to this point it had been assumed that on the estate becoming the property of the University Miss Davies would leave and take up residence elsewhere. But at its meeting on 19 November 1959 the Council was told that Gregynog would be conveyed to the University as soon as possible, but that Miss Davies would continue to live there, paying rent to the University and undertaking full maintenance of the property on an annual tenancy. The Council readily agreed to these new arrangements. On 2 May 1960 a letter was received from Miss Davies's solicitors making the formal offer of Gregynog to the University. The proposals contained in the letter state that 'Miss Davies will as soon as practicable after this offer is accepted convey Gregynog Estate to the University.' Should the University at any time not make use of the property for such educational purposes as had been agreed upon, it would pass to the Margaret Davies Charity. The sum of £12,000 would be made available annually towards the maintenance of the property. Certain furniture and fixtures in the Hall would be made over to the University immediately, and an immediate grant of £10,000 would be made to enable the University to buy such chattels at Gregynog as Miss Davies would be willing to sell. Finally, 'Miss Davies will by insurance or by a provision in her Will or by other appropriate means provide for all estate duty (if any) that may become payable on her death in respect of the Gregynog Estate.' The bequest made, as will be seen, in exceedingly generous terms, was formally accepted by the University Court at its meeting on 20 May 1960. It only remained to affix the Seal of the University to the requisite documents, which were dated 23 May. Thus the University of Wales entered into possession of Gregynog, but not as yet into occupation.

The agreement concerning Miss Davies's tenancy stipulated that she could determine the lease at six months' notice. It was therefore felt that the University should be prepared with ideas and plans which could be put into operation at short notice, if necessary, and a new committee was appointed to have an oversight of matters relating to Gregynog. This was constituted as follows: three representatives of the Council, the Principals of the Colleges and the Provost of the Medical School, and two representatives of the Senate of each constituent institution. The committee prepared a report on the estimated cost of the first stage of development, staffing needs, and the potentialities of the estate and the surrounding area for biological teaching and research.

In order that members of the University might come to know Gregynog and be in a position to envisage possible developments, Miss Davies decided to invite all Heads of Department and their wives to 'open days' at Gregynog on 18 and 30 May 1961. The invitation was accepted by forty-eight Heads of Department.

On 13 March 1963 Miss Davies died. The University took the necessary steps to enable it to make use of Gregynog with as little delay as possible. It was decided to retain all members of the staff who were in posts at the time, and not to disturb existing tenancies. The University Estates Committee was asked to undertake general supervision of the farms and buildings. Estimates of the annual costs were prepared, and the agreement of the constituent institutions was obtained to a proposal that the University should retain £1,000 from the block grant of each College and £500 from that of the Medical School in lieu of charges for accommodation of staff and students attending courses at Gregynog.

The most important step of all was taken at the meeting of the Council on 14 November 1963, when Dr. Glyn Tegai Hughes, lecturer in Comparative Literary Studies at the University of Manchester, was appointed Warden, to take up his duties on 1 April 1964. Thus five years of discussion and planning came to fruition, in the sense that the University of Wales was about to embark on a new enterprise, the like of which it had never experienced before. Some of us who had been closely associated with the project from the start had our moments of anxiety lest the proposals for the development of Gregynog should fail to obtain the support from the Colleges which was indispensable to its success. But we had faith in the Warden's personality and vision, and in the readiness of our colleagues in the Colleges to grasp what was now within their reach, and the events of the succeeding years have fully justified that faith.

CHAPTER ELEVEN

THE UNIVERSITY AT GREGYNOG

GLYN TEGAI HUGHES

THERE were, when the University accepted the bequest of Gregynog, several sceptics. They acknowledged the munificence but doubted the utility. The location was, after all, almost equally unsuitable for all the colleges. The house was not only remote but, to some, forbidding. Would the colleges make full use of any proposed centre, or would the enterprise gradually seep away?

There had, of course, been many consultations with the academic departments. Zoological, botanical, geological and other field courses were elaborated; plans for musical activities were discussed; expansive extra-mural programmes were envisaged. Today these initial proposals bear little detailed relationship to what has evolved; but at the time they played a necessary role in indicating that there were many possible functions for Gregynog, and strengthening the resolve to proceed.

A Gregynog Committee of the University Council was formed under the Chairmanship of Dr. Thomas Parry, then Principal of Aberystwyth (later chairmen have been Dr. F. Llewellyn-Jones and Sir Goronwy Daniel) and at the end of 1963 the present writer was appointed Warden. Shortly afterwards, Mr. Percy Owen was chosen as Bursar and both came to live at Gregynog in the Spring of 1964. By October, the Hall was ready to receive courses.

The first problem for any visitor was to find it. On the very first day a carload drove in from the east and out again to the west without seeing the Hall; they finally arrived after an interesting hour in the lanes. Over the years our signposting has improved, though it is still slightly erratic. The journey by train is perhaps easier, though not if, as in the case of a distinguished speaker, one emerges at Newport, Gwent and asks for a taxi to Gregynog. A very early decision was to avoid calling it Gregynog Hall where possible. It was not going to be easy to describe its function in a phrase (residential conference and educational centre is one formula we use), and it seemed best to try to let the simple name take the strain.

It was also bilingual, as were our internal signs from quite early on. Translation as such was avoided: Y Parlwr Mawr (The Great Parlour) and the Senior Common Room were the same place, as were The Annexe and Y Rhandy Newydd—a name that drew comment. For an Emergency Exit we took a word 'Dihangborth' from the eighteenth century Ellis Wynne.

The house had its difficulties as a centre for larger groups. Six-inch watermains had narrowed to half-an-inch and pressure was low. The Old Servants' Hall had to do duty as a refectory and ran to two temperatures —too hot and too cold; it also seated fewer people than we could sleep, though two more places could be gained by taking the doors off. Electrical equipment was a problem as the supply was at 110V DC, achieved by an elaborate generator bringing it down from the mains 240 AC; there was then a transformer in the cellar bringing the supply back to 240 AC for the television set. Coal for the boilers could not be tipped directly into the boiler house but had to be dumped on the path outside; one man spent most of his working life shovelling it into the hoppers.

All these eccentricities soon vanished, however; with generous assistance from the Trustees of the Gwendoline and Margaret Davies Charities and from the University Grants Committee we rewired, built a new refectory, put in new boilers, laid new mains. Over the years we have tried, as far as possible, to redecorate as if Gregynog were still a private house. The furniture has helped: Peter Waals chairs in the Library, Bryn-mawr pieces in some of the bedrooms, fine Dryad cane chairs in the Music Room. The hospital beds in the attics were less welcome features for some seven or eight years. Then the pictures; if the great paintings are now all in Cardiff, some of the lesser ones passed to the University and others have returned on long loan from the National Museum. There are fine Whistler, John and Zorn prints, two Rodin bronzes—a head of Mahler and a magnificent head and shoulders of Victor Hugo—and two works by the Belgian sculptor, Georges Minne, who was befriended by the Davies family in his period of exile in Montgomeryshire during the first world war.

It was a great good fortune that so many of the staff of Gregynog stayed on after the transfer to the University, and that newcomers fitted in so well. They could not all have approved of the new ways or the new people; but country calm and integrity led them to give us a chance.

In a few ways the changes had been for the better. The sisters' last years had, to some extent, been clouded by illness and a running down of activity. Suddenly there was a great deal more life about the place; there was a little more freedom in the gardens; things were replaced rather than patched. Though when, for the best reasons and with architectural advice, we took the chimneys down, one of the gardeners lamented that it didn't look like a mansion any more.

Granted that we were in business, we now needed to attract custom. A scheme sponsored by Miss Margaret Davies to enable scholars to work at Gregynog for varying periods had been a comprehensive failure, in spite of a formidably distinguished committee's support. Was this due to the location, an inadequate library, or what? Would organised use by student groups suffer the same fate?

Our first pamphlet referred to individual scholars, to research groups, reading parties, summer schools and use by other universities, but made it clear that the main objects were to bring together selected students from parallel departments in the constituent colleges of the University of Wales and 'to relate the specialist instruction to the general cultural background'. One has to admit that not very much of the second objective has survived experience. The general length of courses is about two-and-a-half days and there is not a great deal of time to spare after specialist lectures and seminars. I have warm recollections of a strikingly polite discussion with some foresters to whom I had given a talk on James Joyce, based largely, as I recall, on the famous passage in *Ulysses* where the wedding guests all have arboreal names. Perhaps it is just as well that there was a fairly rapid development to a regular pattern in which a course would choose perhaps a film classic (sometimes related to the topic under discussion), a visit to the Press, a talk or reading by a resident artist or, more rarely, a piano or Lieder recital.

Departmental groups were, at first, not quite sure what to make of the place. What could be achieved in a few days? Would the concentration and the social relationships outweigh the upheaval and the travel? What would the food be like and would the rooms be cold? Historians, philosophers, foresters and statisticians were among the first to sample the product. No harm seemed to come to them and they all wished to return. Within a year or so a regular pattern of visits was established, but the pace then was leisurely and there would be substantial gaps between courses.

It would be optimistic to claim that all courses were equally well organised, nor did all recognise that the primary aim of a weekend was academic rather than recreational. The very rapid growth in demand for dates at Gregynog in the seventies did, however, provide a solution to these relatively minor difficulties. Those few groups that made inadequate use of their time were, unaccountably, not reminded to book for the following year; a very few were more directly told that a year's interval would be wise. The great majority of departmental organisers will, however, go to great trouble with the programme, with sharing out student places, persuading colleagues to give talks, proposing a visiting speaker (and lecturers of great distinction, academic, political, artistic, from very many different countries have been to Gregynog in ten years). Many departments wish that Gregynog were bigger; what a pity it isn't possible to bring sixty rather than fifty, how can we fit all our students in as our departments grow larger? Perhaps this is a compliment; but one feels that, if Gregynog were able to house seventy, there would be some to say 'what a pity it isn't eighty'. The intention, after all, is that there should be selection and a degree of social mingling that becomes more difficult as numbers grow. Observation over the years suggests that the most successful conferences are those that do not use a shoe-horn to fit in their participants.

On a typical weekend there would be perhaps five lectures, each followed by a discussion, though some groups will naturally be doing practical work in the grounds, conducting a crisis game or working in small syndicates. From time to time an organiser will wish to fit in more lectures; settling for fewer usually seems hardly to merit priority bookings.

The house runs, one hopes, on relaxed lines. There are no formalities at meals, no high table, no dress requirements. The aim is that visitors should be comfortable, and they are helped to be considerate by the one firm request—no undue noise late at night. An agreeable feature of the University's occupation is that there has been almost no damage of any importance to the house or its contents. On the whole it does seem to be true that people are likely to look after property that is itself in good order but to help the shoddy towards its doom. This is not to suggest that all visitors approve of Gregynog. Most are, I believe, impressed by its bizarre magnificence externally and by the ordered interior, the works of art, the furniture, the carpets. Some, however, transfer to the University their sense of outrage that it should ever have been owned by an individual. Some find it intolerably rural and remote. Too much should not be made of such dissatisfactions; they tend to be answered by bookings that run well over a year ahead.

Many groups from outside the University of Wales have, of course, used Gregynog. It has, unhappily, become increasingly difficult to find dates for individual departments from other Universities; but a good number still come in association with departments from within the Welsh colleges. Over the years staff and student groups have come from Aston, Birmingham, Bristol, East Anglia, Keele, L.S.E., Liverpool, Manchester, Oxford, York and Karlsruhe. Scores of other Universities would, of course, be represented in any list of visiting scholars and participants in conferences and seminars. Nobel prizewinners and generals, politicians and businessmen, diplomats, novelists, trade unionists, peers, farmer poets, bishops and *Good Food Guide* inspectors (in a non-professional capacity), all these and many others have passed through Gregynog in ten years. The list of non-university bodies that have arranged conferences and courses here is almost equally varied: from the Welsh Arts Council to the Society of Friends, from the Montgomeryshire (and later Powys) Education Authority to Western Command. Courses are arranged with some regularity by the North Wales Arts Association, The Welsh Books Council, The Welsh Education Inspectorate and many other Welsh bodies. In a typical year there will be some twenty such groups with a good number of day visits by other organisations. The University itself also, on occasion, uses Gregynog to entertain distinguished visitors.

The individual scholars who had not been attracted by Miss Davies's scheme did now come, though initially not in large numbers. The late Professor R. F. Treharne and Mrs. Treharne were the first such visitors —visiting readers, as they came to be called. Since then scores have stayed either for days or weeks and two studentships of a month's duration are awarded annually so that some research students may have a similar opportunity. The major portions of two of the late Dr. T. I. Ellis's books were written at Gregynog. The longest stay, and one of the most welcome, was of some five or six months in 1966 by Dr. J. W. Scott, formerly Professor of Philosophy at Cardiff. He was by then eight-seven and was completing his *Synoptic Index to the Proceedings of the Aristotelian Society*. He could have been taught by someone who had listened to Hegel; the dates would have been right but, alas, the names he remembered were not. Nothing, however, could have been better for Gregynog in those early months than such a model of courtesy and rectitude, a link with the Scottish tradition of high-minded academic endeavour coupled with a warm sense of social justice and human brotherhood.

Not the least of Dr. Scott's contributions was one of several hundred volumes from his library. The nature of any library development at Gregynog had been a matter of some concern from the beginning. When the earlier move to offer facilities to readers had been considered by Miss Davies and her advisers, it had been realised that some expansion of the library would be necessary. The *Dictionary of National Biography* had therefore been acquired, but that was about all. There were, however, some thousands of books on the fine arts, gardening and miscellaneous subjects, partly in the Library and partly in bedrooms and elsewhere in the house. The tradition of having a selection of books in bedrooms was clearly one to be retained and these could be considered apart from the Library proper; but what should the general policy be? It would not be possible to compete with College libraries and yet a university institution without a library of some special interest and value seemed to me a poor thing. We decided, therefore, to specialise in the fine arts, music and Celtic and Arthurian studies with a section on typography that would slowly acquire examples of fine printing in addition to the two sets of Gregynog Press books (in the ordinary and special bindings) generously given by Miss Davies. We also built up a general reference section, so that a visiting reader could feel himself reasonably well equipped in this direction, and other books as they happened to come, or as they reflected a somewhat imprecise intention of providing not specialist works in a given field so much as the works in that field which might be found useful by someone in a neighbouring discipline. The testimony from individual scholars is that they find the result helpful and interesting, frequently coming across the unusual book about which they had not known. The Welsh collection was given a good start by purchases from the former Theological College at Bala and by a number of notable gifts. But the building up of the Library has depended a good deal upon diligent searching of antiquarian booksellers' catalogues, of which we receive perhaps a thousand a year. Collections of slides (mainly of paintings and sculptures) and of gramophone records have also been assembled.

Any mention of books in the context of Gregynog brings to mind the Press. When the old company went into voluntary liquidation in 1964, the University was given the opportunity to acquire such equipment and stocks (including the hand-made paper) as had not been taken to the National Library ten years earlier. It was therefore possible to go on binding and we were fortunate in that Mrs. Gwen Edwards, who had worked in the Press bindery, was able to give some time to the binding of books and periodicals for the library. The Albion hand press was also brought into use, either during visits by the College of Librarianship Wales, by the Northern Branch of the Printing Historical Society and others, or during Gregynog's own courses on Research Method for Literary Students.

Groups of visitors were also shown round the Press on innumerable occasions. The usual procedure would be to look at some of the books in the house and then to be shown the equipment in the Press buildings under my inexpert guidance. Occasionally, Dora Herbert Jones, who had been Secretary to the Press, would come over and add authenticity and enthusiasm to the presentation. She was, as many will know, an incomparable expositor and advocate of the highest standards in printing as in so much else, and it is good that her descriptions of the glories of the Press were captured on film by BBC TV. But the Press was still little more than a museum, though we were reluctant to accept this and to mount items on exhibition there. In a desire to make it once again a working Press we asked Derek Nuttall of Chester to prepare a report on its present state and its future possibilities; and out of this grew the University Council's imaginative decision to found a Gregynog Printing Fellowship, whose first holder, Michael Hutchins, is at this moment printing a fine edition of R. S. Thomas's *Laboratories of the Spirit.*

The Press, and his own efforts there, are described with wry affection by the late B. S. Johnson, in an article in *The Private Library.* Bryan Johnson had been the first Gregynog Arts Fellow, the Fellowship having been established in 1969 with the co-operation of the Welsh Arts Council and the University College of Wales, Aberystwyth. Most Fellows are in residence for some four to six months, meeting students and giving lectures, poetry-readings, instrumental recitals, workshop tours or whatever may be appropriate, and getting on with their own work. During his stay here Bryan Johnson wrote the novel *House Mother Normal* and a good number of poems, including a sequence 'Hafod a Hendref', on which a film directed by him and later shown on HTV was based:

> . . . For once in my life I felt secure,
> could work at my limits; physical
> stress symptoms subsided, disappeared . . .
> I became that old absurdity
> a thinking man holding a pencil
> making marks on a sheet of paper
> at a southern window up the bank
> of a reserved valley as near as
> may be to where poetry began.

The second Fellow was the sculptor, Michael Pennie, and the works he produced at Gregynog—many based on the ziggurat—were exhibited both in a Welsh Arts Council Exhibition shown at Aberystwyth, Cardiff, Bangor and Gregynog and in the Angela Flowers Gallery in London. It was during his stay at Gregynog that he began working in wood, a medium to which he has increasingly turned.

He was followed by the distinguished harpist, Osian Ellis, whose recitals were a memorable feature of his tenure. His researches here were mainly on the history of Welsh music and the first fruits of these are to be seen in an important lecture published in the *Transactions of the Cymmrodorion Society 1972 and 1973* (1974). He also organised a weekend festival, which included a recital by Peter Pears, accompanied by Benjamin Britten. The fourth Arts Fellow, Keith Griffiths, produced during his period of residence a twenty minute film, *Ifan ar Ffo,* under the auspices of Bwrdd Ffilmiau Cymraeg. At Ruthin in 1973 it played a distinguished part in the first presentation of Welsh films at the National Eisteddfod. His successor, Tony Harrison, was busily engaged on his translation of Racine's *Phèdre* for the National Theatre (published as *Phaedra Britannica,* London, 1975), but also wrote a good number of other translations and original poems. Our sixth Fellow, Emyr Humphreys, worked on the third in his new series of novels, of which *National Winner* and *Flesh and Blood* have already been published. Then, in September 1975, we welcomed the painter, Jack Crabtree, who had just spent a year on a commission by the National Coal Board to illustrate pit life, often underground. Many of the drawings then made he is here using as a starting-point for paintings. The Fellows, and in many cases their family, have enlivened the underlying intellectual and creative climate of Gregynog a good deal, and meeting them has been a rewarding experience for many visitors. Most of them, too, have retained their links and revisit us from time to time.

In many cases the Fellows also had their work brought to the attention of local people, by exhibitions, recitals or lectures. Two literary societies (Cylch Llenyddol Maldwyn and The Montgomeryshire Literary Group) meet regularly at Gregynog. Their meetings are arranged in association with the North Wales Arts Association and, over the years, they have been addressed by almost all the leading literary figures in Wales and many from outside. Here, too, the Fellows have played their part. Exhibitions, some of work by Fellows (or in one case, by the Fellow's wife) have been held regularly in the Music Room, and we have bought pictures from them as resources permitted.

The Gregynog Choir remained in existence for a while, and Professor Ian Parrott generously gave his time to conduct it; but the lack of men (our gardening staff had, after all, declined from twenty-six to eight) was too much of a handicap and it faded quietly from the scene.

Concerts have been arranged with some regularity, though not perhaps as frequently as might have been desirable. We have, in addition to the Pears-Britten concert, heard Margaret Price, Rafael Orozco, Malcolm Binns and a number of quartets and choirs. We ourselves have not ventured an open-air concert, but there have been one or two striking ones arranged in the grounds by the County Youth Orchestra. Several mixed media shows have been put on; one on dreams, and one during the National Eisteddfod of 1965 'Y Ddau Chwyldro', of which one sprightly critic wrote: 'For the literary sophisticates a remarkable session at Gregynog Hall was the top event. This consisted of a kind of Ph.D. thesis set to music, under the title of "The Two Revolutions". The object was to show the relation between Methodism in Wales and the Romantic Movement in Europe. Since the programme did not begin until after 11 p.m. and was partly in French and German as well as Welsh and English, the cream of the Welsh intelligentsia who had gathered at Gregynog got somewhat clotted before it was over.' (*London Welshman,* XX, 8 (Sept. 1965). p. 1.)

Any successes achieved at Gregynog in recent years are for others to judge. For my part I wish that we had done more in the way of musical activities and art courses, and that we had arranged more courses of our own, particularly perhaps to explain Wales to overseas visitors. We look forward to developing in these directions and in the attracting of more individual scholars and research groups. We are not in competition with Gregynog's past, but we should perhaps try to surround ourselves with more visual evidence of our own generation's creativity.

Gregynog still has a special function to fulfil in Welsh society. Its historical roots lie in a period when there was an easy commerce between different sections of society; in the days of the Blayneys it was the kind of great house that remained close to the soil and the surrounding community. The two Davies sisters opened up Gregynog to wider European influences, in music, in their international conferences, by their art collection. At the same time they attempted, with surprising success in the case of the Press, to create a craft tradition that would enrich national life.

What a university institution should be able to do is to nourish these different strands. The sense of the past may not quiver for all who come to Gregynog; but, for some at any rate, the ideals of a unified but receptive society may glow through its history.

SELECT BIBLIOGRAPHY
(see also bibliography to Chapter on 'The Gregynog Press')

HUGHES, T. W., 'Gregynog: its History and Associations', *The Montgomeryshire Society Year Book 1935–6*, pp. 37–41; 3 illus.

INGAMELLS, JOHN, *The Davies Collection of French Art*, Cardiff, National Museum of Wales, 1967, xiv, 113 pp.; 8 colour and 75 half-tone plates.

JOHNSON, B. S., 'The Gregynog Press and the Gregynog Fellowship', *Private Library*, 2nd ser., vi, 1 (Spring 1973), 4–15; 4 illus.

JONES, THOMAS, *A Diary with Letters 1931–1950*, London, Oxford U.P., 1954, xlv, 582 pp.

JONES, THOMAS, *Whitehall Diary*, edited by Keith Middlemass, London, Oxford U.P., vol. I, 1916–1925, 1969, xxiv, 358 pp.; vol. II, 1926–1930, 1969, xiii, 311 pp.

OWEN, W. SCOTT, *The History of Gregynog*, typescript 1888, 180 pp. In the possession of Lord Sudeley; copies at Gregynog and the National Library of Wales.

OWEN, W. SCOTT, 'Arthur Blayney and his Home, Gregynog Hall', *Montgomeryshire Collections*, xxv (1891), 105–14.

OWEN, W. SCOTT, 'Parochial History of Tregynon', *Montgomeryshire Collections*, xxx (1896), 1–168.

PARROTT, IAN, *The Spiritual Pilgrims*, Llandybie, C. Davies, 1969, 196 pp.; 16 plates.

[PERKIN, GEORGE], 'Early Welsh Cottages', *Concrete Quarterly*, 95 (Oct.-Dec. 1972), pp. 26–30.

ROWLEY-MORRIS, E., 'The Family of Blayney', *Montgomeryshire Collections*, xxi (1887), 273–302 and xxii (1888), 71–110.

SANDFORD, GEORGE, 'The House of Gregynog, The Blayneys and the Hanbury-Tracys, Lords Sudeley', *Montgomeryshire Collections*, xviii (1885), 229–44.

SUDELEY, LORD, 'Gregynog before the Year 1900', *Montgomeryshire Collections*, lxii, 2 (1971, issued June 1973), 166–82.

SUDELEY, LORD, 'Toddington and the Tracys', *Transactions of the Bristol and Gloucestershire Archaeological Society*, lxxxviii (1969), 127–72.

THOMAS, IVOR, *Top Sawyer. A biography of David Davies of Llandinam*, London, Longmans, 1938, xvi, 355 pp.

TIPPING, H. AVRAY, 'The Carved Parlour of Gregynog', *Country Life*, 22 Nov. 1919, pp. 668–9; 4 figs.

YORKE, PHILIP, *The Royal Tribes of Wales*, new ed. by Richard Williams, Liverpool, 1887, pp. 155–9.

Particulars of the Gregynog Estate, 1894. For Sale by Private Contract. Debenham, Tewson, Farmer and Bridgewater, Land Agents, London, 19 pp.

Greg-y-Nog Estate, Newtown, Montgomeryshire. For Sale by Auction, 28, 29, 30 and 31 October 1913, at the Town Hall, Newtown, Millar, Son & Co., London, 192 pp.

GREGYNOG IN POETRY

For Welsh Poetry see ROBERTS, ENID, *Braslun o Hanes Llên Powys*, Dinbych, Gee, 1965, 113 pp. (=Astudiaethau Bangor, 2) and notes to the Chapter 'The Blayney Period'.

COLEMAN, ELLIOTT, 'Festival: Gregynog', in his *An American in August-Land*, Chapel Hill, U. of North Carolina P., 1940, pp. 59–60.

DARWALL, MRS. [MARY], formerly Miss Whately, 'Written on walking in the woods of Gregynog in Montgomeryshire', in her *Original Poems on Several Occasions*, London, 1764; reprinted Gregynog Press, June 1924, from 1794 ed.

JOHNSON, B. S., 'Hafod a Hendref', *Planet*, 10 (Feb.-Mar. 1972), pp. 47–54.

MATTHEWS, TOM, 'Concrete Cottages', *The Honest Ulsterman*, 46–47 (Nov. 1974–Feb. 1975), p. 8.

PACEY, PHIL, 'Gregynog', *Clw*, iv, 2 (Summer 1969), 34–5.

INDEX